PRAY
the
WORD

Scribble City
PUBLICATIONS

DEDICATION

To the tears of joy that has continued to flow
The tears of the remembrance of the agony at the Cross
The joyful tears of taking part in that agony
The tears that will be overtaken by joy in heaven
The tears that will be no more to the Glory of God

ACKNOWLEDGEMENTS

I must first give thanks to God, for the strength He made available to me and for the inspiration and close guidance of the Holy Spirit, to be able to put these prayers together within a short space of time.

I am also grateful to those who went out of their way to help. May God bless you all in Jesus' name.

CONTENTS

Prelude

PRAY THE WORD

God never fails to fulfil His Word, except when it is hindered by sin or spoken without faith. For the Word to guarantee answer in prayers, there is need to adhere to its correct application and requirements

Why the Word
This Chapter explains why every single prayer in this Prayer Book is based on the **Word of God** or derived from it. It highlights its greater effectiveness in achieving answers to prayers.

The Word means the Word of God as it is written in the Bible in John 1:1. Matthew 24:35 reads: "Heaven and earth shall pass away, but my words shall not pass away." 'The Word' is immortal, everlasting. It is the living water you drink, and you never thirst again (John 4:13–14). This is the same Word that brings salvation and eternal life. It regenerates the mind spiritually as you get deeply acquainted with it. This is when the power is mostly felt.

"Then said Jesus to these Jews which believed on Him, 'If ye continue in my word, then are ye my disciples indeed' " (John 8:31).

Jesus would prefer us to use His Words exhaustively in everything we do on; think His Word, speak His Word, pray His Word, and live His Word. It is the truth about everything and sanctifies. John 17:17 reads: "Sanctify them through thy truth: thy word is truth." 1 Timothy 4:5 reads: "For it is sanctified by the word of God and prayer." When you pray according to the Word, the result is answered prayers and sanctification. Prayers according to the Word offered with thanksgiving can make any defiled food to be sanctified and can also minister healing and deliverance. Psalm 107:20 reads, "He sent His word, and healed them, and delivered them from their destructions."

Psalm 19:14 reads: "Let the words of my mouth, and the meditation of my heart, be acceptable in thy sight, O LORD, my strength, and my redeemer." It is the reproduction of the Word of God in our hearts through our mouths that enhances answers to our prayers. If you pray according to the Word of God, you cannot pray against His will. Praying the Word is a safeguard from praying against God's will. The scripture in Hebrews 4:12–13 reads:

"For the word of God is quick, and powerful, and sharper than any two edged sword, piercing even to the dividing asunder of soul and spirit, and of the joints and marrow, and is a discerner of the thoughts and intents of the heart. "Neither is there any creature that is not manifest in its sight; but all things are naked and opened unto the eyes of him with whom we have to do." This means that the Word is comprehensive and covers all aspects of human life; its joys and sorrows. It provides solutions to all the problems we can experience. We can always find the scripture that relates to our problems in the Word.

John 12:48–49 reads:
"He that rejecteth me and receiveth not my words, hath one that judgeth him: the word that I have spoken, the same shall judge him in the last day. For I have not spoken of myself; but the Father which sent me, He gave me a commandment of what I should say, and what I should speak." If the Word will judge us in the end, and the Word was put into Jesus's mouth by His Father, Him to whom all prayers and supplications are made, then we have prayed aright when we pray the Word.

The Word is the Son of God, the Second in the God Head, by whom everything in this earth is created.
John 1:1 reads: "In the beginning was the Word, and the Word was with God, and the Word was God."

The solutions to all human problems can be found in the Word. This same Word by which redemption is given to us has already defeated all problems at the Cross.

What this means is that the safest means of achieving

answered prayers is to pray through the Word of God. The Word is the One whom the Almighty God, who created heaven and earth and all that is within and without it, was making reference to when He cautioned Joshua and mankind in Joshua 1:8–9, to the effect that it must not depart from our mouths, but that we should read, speak, meditate, memorize, and act on all that is in It. He went on to say that it is the only way to success and prosperity.

This book of the law was what was available then. It incorporated Joshua's writing. What God, in essence, is saying is that anytime we open our mouths to speak; only things pertaining to the Word should be allowed to proceed. It is the same Word of which Jesus said in John 6:36 that it is life and spirit. If the spirit in the Word activates your request, it can be answered easily. It is the Word that defeated sin and will always defeat Satan for you; and usher you into the Kingdom of God.

The Word sanctifies (Timothy 4:5).
 It cleanses us (John 15:3).
 It heals (Psalm 107:20).
The Word is the same light that guides (Psalm 119:105).
It will make your spiritual and physical progress easier (James 3:2).
It will eliminate all demonic delays and distractions (1 John 3:8.)
It is the Word that teaches and instructs (Psalm 119:130).
It brings prosperity (Joshua 1:8).

We cannot afford not to pray according to the Word. 1 John 5:7 reads: "For there are three that bear record in heaven, the Father, the Word, and the Holy Ghost: and these three are one." Revelation 19:13 reads: "And he was clothed with a vesture dipped in blood: and his Name is called The Word of God."

Each time Jesus prayed for anyone, God usually answered. The same Jesus, the Living Word, has assured us in John 15:7 that "if ye abide in me, and my words abide in you, ye shall ask what ye will, and it shall be done unto you." We experience the problems of unanswered prayers mostly because His Words do not abide in us, and we do not pray according to His will, which is this Word. We would rather pray according to our own will and desires. Some have even used the scriptural passage in Isaiah 45:11 to prove that you can command God in prayers, which is not right. It reads: "Thus saith the LORD, the Holy One of Israel, and his Maker, 'Ask of me the things to come concerning my sons, and concerning the work of my hands command me.' "

Command prayers should be presented with fear, reverence, and obedience. This passage was used by God to draw back the backsliding Israelites, who then had no fear of Him, from their sins of idolatry.

I cannot perceive myself commanding God in prayers because it lacks fear and reverence. God's level of wisdom and knowledge is such that we shall end up making fun of ourselves if we form a habit of sending command prayers to Him, who is already aware of all our problems on this earth. Keep Holy. Just give Him back His Word, humbly and reverently as they relate to your problems. Since the Word guarantees answers to your prayers, then you have to pray according to its requirements. God never fails to fulfil His Word, except where sin abides. Moreover, if you truly fear God, you will be ill at ease to command Him.

This Prayer Book is a good encouragement to those who cannot memorize the Word of God easily. As they read the Word and pray these prayers, their faith in God will be activated. They will believe that they will receive answers, and will receive them (Mark 11:24).

The idea to write this prayer book came as a result of firstly writing a few prayers based solely on the ministration of the Word. Before I knew it, I had compiled a hundred and fifty prayers which I prayed every week on Sunday evenings.

On one faithful midnight while I was praying, I had a sudden spiritual Visitor. He took the prayers, glanced at them, and nodded His head in agreement wearing a good smile as if recalling something. He suddenly disappeared as He came. I made a mental note to endeavour to pray those prayers more often than I was doing. When I had the urge to do a prayer book, I remembered that visitation and decided to write something based solely on the Word of God. When Jesus encountered a face to face confrontation with Satan, it was the Word that He used on those three specific occasions to dismiss him immediately.

This prayer book will in no small measure enhance your chances of having your prayers answered provided you are not living in any known sins which you have not genuinely repented of. I have prayed and asked God while writing this book, not to allow any prayer against His will to be included in it.

When you allow the Word to pray for you, you are led to learn the requirements of that Word and how to fulfil it. When you base your prayer on the Word, your faith in God is activated because His Word is His will. Those who cannot commit the Word to memory can now read it out before saying the prayers.

Since it is the Word that will judge mankind in the end, it is better to familiarize ourselves with it, and humbly give God His Word as we pray.

This prayer book is based on the New Testament Covenant of forgiveness and repentance of sin. As a special mark of reverence to God, the word, 'please' is attached to every prayer.

Some of these prayers were either imparted into me by the Holy Spirit or derived directly from the Word of God.

When I was writing this prayer book, a divine figure told me that he will use it to reach out to some specific individuals. It is not necessarily the length of time spent on the prayers that matters, but the intensity and concentration given to them. Jesus said in Matthew 6:7 "But when ye pray, use not vain repetitions, as the heathens do: for they think that they shall be heard for their much speaking. Be not ye therefore like unto them: for Your Father knoweth what things ye have need of, before ye ask him." Jesus said in Matthew 27:14b that the Scribes and Pharisees, "for a pretence make long prayers".

When you pray, try and be specific and get to the point. Do not spend most of the time whipping up emotion over sins you know that you are not prepared to give up, either because of dishonesty or lack faith in the ability of the Holy Spirit to guide you out of them. There is also a possibility that by so doing, we can provoke the wrath of God. It is not necessarily the physical exercise you perform, the too much noise you make, or the length of time spent while praying that will guarantee answers to the prayers. A contrite, humble, and genuinely repentant heart, totally based on the will of God, will appeal more to the LORD. It is advisable to either stand or kneel down while you pray, provided you do not fall asleep on your knees like me, only to open your eyes and discover that it is the early hours of the morning. It has happened to me, and I felt very sorry for myself when I woke up. I decided to start another session of prayers immediately. On one occasion when I was praying, sitting down, a voice suddenly said, 'I prefer your standing up'.

There was another occasion when I suddenly came to God in prayers over a matter I considered very urgent. He replied, 'I have a routine.' This means that there are guidelines and procedures for presenting prayers to Him. The timing is also His to decide, not yours.

Chapter 1

HINDRANCES AGAINST PRAYERS

Lack of Repentance/Forgiveness

Forgiveness is an essential nature of God which He imparts to human beings to enable them to receive the grace of salvation. Without it, we will all come under His condemnation. Before doing these prayers, it is always very necessary to remember what the Word says about repentance and forgiveness.

The level of your repentance is indicative of your level of holiness and faith. This is because repentance shows total confidence in the power of God to put things right for you, and a willingness to separate yourself from sin.

Proverbs 28:13 reads:
"He that covereth his sins shall not prosper: but whoso confesseth and forsaketh them shall have mercy." How can the Holy Spirit operate in you if you are still carrying your former misdeeds? You are indirectly driving Him away.

If you have no forgiveness for others in your nature, you will not have forgiveness from God, and your requests may not be granted. Matthew 6:14 reads:

"For if ye forgive men their trespasses, your heavenly Father will also forgive you: but if ye forgive not men their trespasses, neither will your Father forgive your trespasses." In the New Testament, all the works of healing and miracles which Jesus performed were done after He had forgiven the victims their sins. So it is today. You must pray the prayer of forgiveness to clear the way before presenting your request to God.

Numbers 14:18 reads: "The LORD is longsuffering, and of great mercy, forgiving iniquity and transgression." Our Lord's Prayer in Matthew 6:12 reads: "And forgive us our debts, as we forgive our debtors".

Forgiveness is a prerequisite to answered prayers. When we forgive genuinely, we do not think or make reference to it in our conversations any more. Most of us, like me, are not finding this easy although it is a necessity, but we shall succeed in Jesus' Name.

Matthew 18:21–22 reads: "Then came Peter to Him, and said, 'Lord, how oft shall my brother sin against me, and I forgive him? Till seven times?' Jesus saith unto him, 'I say not unto thee, until seven times: but, until seventy times seven.' " By the time you have forgiven somebody four hundred and ninety times, you must have formed the habit of forgiving. Mark 11:25 reads:

"And when ye stand praying, forgive, if ye have ought

against any: that your Father also which is in heaven may forgive you your trespasses."

Also, remember that you should not be ashamed to do a heartfelt confession of sins, and work towards not repeating them again. If you slip, do not give up, start from the beginning until you get out of that sin.

Isaiah cried in Isaiah 6:5 saying:

"Woe is me! For I am undone; because I am a man of unclean lips, and I dwell in the midst of a people of unclean lips". He repented genuinely.

David cried to Nathan in shame and agony in 2 Samuel 12:13 and said,

"I have sinned against the Lord." He repented and bore the consequences like a true child of God.

The sins we should ask forgiveness for should at least cover the following areas:

Anger - Ephesians 4:3

Bitterness - Hebrews 12:15

Blasphemy - 2 Timothy 3:2

Covetousness - Hebrews 13:5

Deceit - Romans 3:13

Disobedience - Romans 5:19

Distractions - 1 Corinthians 7:35

Drunkenness - Luke 21:34

Lack of Love - Revelation 2:4

Envy - Acts 17:5

Laziness - Ecclesiastes 10:18

Speaking evil - 1 Peter 2:1

Foolishness - Proverbs 24:9

Evil thought - Proverbs 30:32
Gossip - 1 Timothy 5:13
Greed - Isaiah 56:11
Lies - Proverbs 14:25
Hatred - Proverbs 10:12
Malice - 1 Peter 2:1
Judgment - Romans 14:10
Murder - Matthew 19:18
Idolatry - 1 Corinthians 10:14
Murmuring - 1 Corinthians 10:10
Ungratefulness - 2 Timothy 3:2
Partiality - James 2:3–4
Inordinate affection - Colossians 3:5
Pride - 1 John 2:16
Jealousy - Song 8:6
Rebellion - 1 Samuel 15:23
Stealing - Exodus 20:15
Strife - James 3:16
Sexual Immorality - 1 Corinthians 5:1
Talkativeness - Titus 1:10
Unforgiveness - Mark 11:25–26
Witchcraft - 1 Samuel 15:23

God's will is His Word. If you are doing the will of God, which is obeying the Word of God, whenever you pray with the Word, you will receive good answers to your prayers. If the answer does not come immediately, exercise some patience. He may be working out something better for you. Hebrews 10:36 says,
"For ye have need of patience, that, after ye have done

the will of God, you might receive the promise."

Jeremiah 33:3 reads:
"Call unto me, and I will answer thee, and shew thee great and mighty things, which thou knowest not."
God will not only release the answer we are asking for, but will reveal to us other useful and hidden information pertaining to that problem that will guide us in the future.

Lack of Faith:

Always exercise your faith in prayers since the scripture in Hebrews 11:6 has warned that without faith, it is difficult to please Him. This means that any prayer that is said without faith cannot please God. Christ Himself said in Matthew 21:22 "And all things, whatsoever ye shall ask in prayer, believing, ye shall receive." If you do not believe, you do not receive. If you do not have the faith in the ability of God to do that which you are asking, He will not answer that prayer.

Sin:

The Word of God in Isaiah 59:1–2 has said it all. It reads:
"Behold, the LORD's hand is not shortened, that it cannot save; neither his ear heavy, that it cannot hear: but your iniquities have separated between you and your God, and your sins have hid his face from you, that he will not hear."
Isaiah 1:15 in support of these facts reads:
"And when ye spread forth your hands, I will hide mine

eyes from you; yea, when ye make many prayers, I will not hear."

The matter of sin deserves the seriousness it calls for, so that when we pray, we do not blame God for not answering. Many people focus on His mercy instead of on how to give up the sin.

What we lose sight of is the fact that He cannot compromise His goodness. His eyes cannot behold iniquity; therefore, you have to sort out yourself well before coming to Him in prayers. He did not compromise His goodness because of the pain that Jesus was experiencing on the Cross: remember that cry, "My God, My God, why hast thou forsaken me?" This was because of the sin of the world placed on Him. At that point in time, He had to turn His eyes away from His Beloved Son. It is not that He is not able to answer, but that His eyes which cannot behold sin will automatically be turned away from the sinner. If Satan has gained the greater part of you, remember that the solution is repentance, confession, and remittance of sins. The prayer of a sinner is an abomination in His eyes. This means that the prayer is proceeding from the territory of Satan. Immediately it is presented, He quickly turns His face away from the abomination. The seriousness of this matter has already been emphasized, Brethren. You will remember that according to the scriptures, Jesus always forgave before He healed. On a specific occasion, He warned the man He healed to sin no more, lest a worse evil come upon him. He has to forgive you first before

He can do anything worthwhile for you.

God's Word with regards to sin is that we should eject it immediately from our lives at all costs. We should ignore the provocations and attacks of Satan, and concentrate on the work of being spotless like Him.

There was a time in my life when I thought that I was working tirelessly for the Lord in spite of all provocations. On one occasion, I travelled to another town for an official duty. I was feeling very bad about a serious act of discrimination against me in the church. In the night, the Lord opened my eyes to perceive just His two hands which were whiter than snow and very spotless. What terrified me was their sheer size. As I was observing this, I was imagining their expanse and wandering whether this was larger than the city I was in. Then it passed away. The lesson it conveyed was that I should forgive and occupy my mind and time with how to clean up myself, get those sins off me instead of wasting time, sorrowing over what people were doing to me. He is saying, I cannot see those problems because of your sin, let alone solve them. There is nothing worse than sin in the life of anybody whether it is pride, selfishness, unforgiveness, anger, etc. Sin is sin and it's either repented off or punished. May God have mercy on us in Jesus' name.

Lack Of Praises and Worship:

God will like us to start our prayers with praises and worship; it makes Him happy because that is a major reason why we are created. Revelation 4:11 reads:

"Thou art worthy, O Lord, to receive glory and honour and power: for thou hast created all things, and for thy pleasure they are and were created." We are created to give pleasure, not sorrow to God.

We are also told that God inhabits the praises of His people. It is when He inhabits your praises and thanksgiving that He will be better disposed to answer your prayers. If many groups of people are praying and one group is happily praising and worshipping Him, His attention may first quickly be drawn to them if not for anything but firstly, to enjoy their songs and praises. Hebrews 13:15 puts it this way:
"By him therefore let us offer the sacrifice of praise to God continually, that is, the fruit of our lips giving thanks to his name." Psalm 34:1 opens with the following words: "I will bless the LORD at all times: His praise shall continually be in my mouth."

In Psalm 98:4, the Psalmist says,
"Make a joyful noise unto the LORD, all the earth: make a loud noise, and rejoice, and sing praise."
Psalm 95:1–2 reads:
"O come, let us sing unto the LORD: let us make a joyful noise to the rock of our salvation.
"Let us come before his presence with thanksgiving, and make a joyful noise unto him with Psalm." The best way to come to God in prayer is with praises, worship, and thanksgiving.

Not Praying in Tongues

If you speak in the tongue of the Holy Spirit, you are advised to do so during these prayers. If you are not sure that your tongue is from the Holy Spirit, be advised not to speak it. 1 Corinthians 14:15 reads:

"What is it then? I will pray with the spirit, and I will pray with the understanding also: I will sing with the spirit, and I will sing with the understanding also."

It is very spiritually rewarding. Romans 8:26–27 says,

"Likewise the Spirit also helpeth our infirmities: for we know not what we should pray for as we ought: but the Spirit itself maketh intercession for us with groanings which cannot be uttered.

"And he that searcheth the hearts knoweth what is the mind of the Spirit, because he maketh intercession for the saints according to the will of God."

This is God, the Holy Spirit, the third in command in Heaven, interceding for us according to the will of God which is the Word of God. We are told that GOD knows what is in the mind of the Spirit because His intercessions are according to His Word which is His will. This means that any prayer that is not according to the Word of God is already discredited. This is why this prayer book is solely based on the Word of God.

Not Aligning Yourself to the Word:

It is necessary to make sure that your prayer is aligned to the Word of God. When I finished from the school of Ministry, which was considered the highest and most challenging in the Bible College I attended, God spoke to me when I was doing my practicals. He said, 'Do not tell them what you do not do.' On another occasion, He said, 'Tell them what is in the Word.' I was terrified because sometimes I said what I was not doing, like not being selfish. This was about seventeen years ago. Sometimes, I had to let the audience know that I too was also struggling with that particular sin. I then realized that I had to be strictly guided by the Word as far as God is concerned.

Brethren, the Word of God is one of the armours which He gave to us to wear for protection against the enemy (Ephesians 6:13). It is called the Sword of the Spirit. Ephesians 6:17 reads:

"And take the helmet of salvation and the sword of the spirit, which is the word of God". We have to put it on every morning before leaving our homes by praying with it and studying it.

Lack of Fasting:

Fasting is the twin-born of serious prayers. Some prayers just can't move without it. It is a necessity where there is threat of death or serious infirmity. The Psalmist said in Psalm 35:13:

"But as for me, when they were sick, my clothing was sackcloth: I humbled my soul with fasting".

Fasting helps you to approach God with humility. There are problems that cannot just go unless they are confronted with fasting and prayers. Jesus gave an example of one in the case of the lunatic boy. Fasting boosts up our faith, so that when we pray, we generate greater confidence and faith. Matthew 17:19–21 reads:

"Then came the disciples to Jesus apart, and said, why could not we cast him out? And Jesus said unto them, because of your unbelief: for verily I say unto you, if ye have faith as a grain of mustard seed, ye shall say unto this mountain, remove hence to yonder place; and it shall remove; and nothing shall be impossible unto you. Howbeit this kind goeth not out but by prayer and fasting." If His disciples had fasted, they would have generated enough faith in their prayers for God to be able to drive away the evil spirit. How long or often you fast depend on the seriousness of the problem. In order to get fasting to work, you have to fast aright.

The Word of God has given us the guidelines for fasting which we must keep. You can find this in Matthew 6:16–18 and it reads:

"Moreover when ye fast, be not, as the hypocrite, of a sad countenance: for they disfigure their faces, that they may appear unto men to fast. Verily I say unto you, they have their reward. But thou, when thou fastest, anoint thy head, and wash thy face; that thou appear not unto men to fast, but unto thy Father which is in secret: and thy Father, which seeth in secret, shall reward thee openly." Isaiah 58:6–7, 9 reads:

"Is not this the fast that I have chosen? to loose the bands of wickedness, to undo the heavy burdens, and to let the oppressed go free, and that ye break every yoke? Is it not to deal thy bread to the hungry, and that thou bring the poor that are cast out to thy house? when thou seest the naked, that thou cover him; and that thou hide not thyself from thine own flesh?

"Then shalt thou call and the LORD shall answer; thou shalt cry and he shall say, here I am."

Have you been praying for a long time without receiving answers to your prayers? Check yourself again to ascertain whether the Lord is waiting for you to approach Him appropriately.

Lack of Reverence for God:

You will observe that almost all these prayers have the word 'please' attached to them. This is done as an act of reverence and total recognition of the supremacy and authority of God. A servant is never greater than the master; therefore, you cannot command God to do anything, unless you want to answer your prayers yourself. You have to plead with Him, in humility, respect, and love. In the Old Testament, Moses, David, Hezekiah, and even Ahab, tore their clothes, put ashes on themselves, and fell on the ground when they presented serious requests before Him. All their prayers were answered.

James 4:9–10 (NKJV) reads:

"Lament and mourn and weep! Let your laughter be turned to mourning and your joy to gloom. Humble yourselves in the sight of the Lord, and He will lift you up."

21

Lack of Love:

Do not invite the spirit of death while you are praying to come and *terminate the life of any human being created in the image of God*. After working for you, that terrible spirit, who has no friends, may decide to turn against you or any member of your family. Therefore, try as much as possible to avoid praying for the death of any human being when you pray. This area is God's prerogative. Try and generate as much love as you can in your prayers.

It was not easy for some of us often confronted by unrepentant eaters of flesh and drinkers of human blood who swore that they would never repent or give up. These ones spend their time digging one pit after another and setting up one padlock after the other. One day, the Lord opened my eyes, and I saw in the spirit, something as large as a small hut of the enemy in clusters, together. I looked again and realized that they were all padlocks. I then realized how desperate the enemy could really get, and the truth of the scripture in Zechariah 4:6 (NKJV) which reads: "Not by might nor by power, but by my Spirit,' says the LORD of hosts."

Try to understand why that enemy is attacking you. They are doing the work of their master, Satan. If God, through your prayers, notices that your hatred is directed towards that person and not his sins, He may refuse to answer you until you repent. This is why some prayers in this book make a distinction between those enemies that have refused adamantly to repent, and those that can repent.

Jesus prayed in Luke 23:34 for those who were almost about to nail Him to the cross saying, "Father, forgive them, for they know not what they do." This was in order that the will of God for His life be fulfilled.

Stephen prayed in Acts 7:60 for those who were already terminating his life with stones saying, "Lord, lay not this sin to their charge." David commanded the man who slew Saul, his worst enemy, to be killed instantly. The man thought that he did David a great favour. It is quite amazing, the extent that the Saints went after the pattern of Christ in order to align their prayers to the will of God. We do not have much of the challenges they had today.

Are you ashamed to confess to people that God does not answer your prayers? Have you completely lost hope in the fact that your problems can be solved through prayers? Check again the conditions for getting prayers answered. Amend your ways promptly. You are not far from answered prayers this time around. Just pray the Word of God into your requests. You can pray them as often and as long as you wish until answers are received. God honours His Word. In John 15:3, Jesus said: "Now ye are clean through the word which I have spoken unto you." The word from the mouth of the Lord had already ministered sanctification and deliverance to His disciples. They needed no other for the moment, except when the Holy Spirit will replace Him at His resurrection. This is the power of the Word that will also minister answered prayers to our requests if we sincerely pray according to it.

Chapter 2

PRAISE AND WORSHIP

Praise and worship are rendered in advance to God as an act of faith. God inhabits the praises of His people. It encourages Him to look into their prayers provided that all requirements are met.

Psalm 100:2, 4 reads:
"Serve the LORD with gladness: come before his presence with singing. Enter into his gates with thanksgiving, and into his courts with praise; be thankful unto him, and bless his name."

We learn as we grow. On one occasion, when I was asking the Lord for something on a continuous basis, He asked me whether I had thanked Him for all those things He had already done, pertaining to that very matter. I was ashamed because He had truly done a lot. It is when you thank Him for what He had done that He will be happy to do more.

Praise and worship show that we are appreciative of all

He is doing and can make Him happily disposed towards us. The Bible tells us that all creations of God have to praise Him always. In fact, everything that moves owes Him praises and thanksgiving.

Psalm 69:34 reads:
"Let the heaven and the earth praise him, the seas, and every thing that moveth therein."
Psalm 150:6 reads:
"Let every thing that hath breath praise the LORD. Praise ye the LORD."
Psalm 138:1 reads:
"I will praise thee with my whole heart: before the gods will I sing praise unto thee."

Psalm 47:7 reads:
"For God is the King of all the earth: sing ye praises with understanding."

You have to praise Him in the right way. You can also sing songs and hymns; do any form of praise and worship that will make Him happy, that will enhance the answering of your prayers once you are sure that you are not living in any conscious sin; otherwise, your entire request should be centred with praises on developing a true spirit of repentance and forgiveness of sins. Most people have had their prayers answered by only praising and thanking God.

There was something marvellous, which the Lord did

for me that made me to proclaim Him as a God of great excellence, perfection, and high standards, while testifying. In order to show appreciation, I then decided to do a vigil of worship, praise, and thanksgiving, from midnight to six in the morning. I really enjoyed it and felt a bit relieved.

As you praise Him also, centre your thoughts on the words you are saying or singing. Let it not be said of you by God that these people honoureth me with their lips but their hearts are far away from me (Mark 7:6).

As you praise God with these scriptures, let your heart speak them out with genuine love and appreciation. You may even get an okay before you get into the main body of the requests provided that you also handle the plea for forgiveness in an honest manner. Remember that we are supposed to praise Him in righteousness.

Start this prayer like this:
Holy Father, merciful, kind, and loving, I approach You with a genuine heart-felt appreciation for all You have done for us, sinners. I thank You for the power of the Holy Spirit, the Blood of ransom, our lives, protection, health, healing touch, provision, training, etc. I thank You most importantly for salvation and eternal life. Please accept my thanks in Jesus' name.

Thank Him also for all those unusual specific acts of miracles, signs, and wonders that He has performed in

your life and that of your family in the Name of Jesus.
Now, after each Bible quotation, you pray the prayer that
follows. Make sure that you read out the Bible quotations!

Psalm 18:50 reads:
"Great deliverance giveth he to his king; and sheweth
mercy to his anointed, to David, and his seed for
evermore."
I will sing praises unto Thy name, Jehovah God, for Your
mercy endureth forever. You delivered our souls from
death and from the continuous attacks against us.
You are the same yesterday, today and forever. Be thou
glorified in Jesus' Name.

Psalm 18:48–49 reads:
"He delivereth me from mine enemies: yea, thou liftest
me up above those that rise up against me: thou hast
delivered me from the violent man. Therefore will I give
thanks unto thee, O LORD, among the heathen, and sing
praises unto thy name."
Thou, Holy God of Power, that has delivered us and is
still delivering us from our enemies, may glory, honour,
dominion, power, and thanksgiving, remain with You,
in the Name of Jesus.

Psalm 50:14–15 reads:
"Offer unto God thanksgiving; and pay thy vows unto
the most High: and call upon me in the day of trouble: I
will deliver thee, and thou shalt glorify me."
O Holy covenant-keeping God, who delivers us from

the wicked because we trust in You, be Thou magnified always in Jesus' Name. Receive honour, thanksgiving, adoration love, and service in Jesus' Name.

The Bible made us to understand in 2 Chronicles 20:22 that it was at that point in time, when Jehoshaphat and his army, drawn from both Judah and Jerusalem, started praising God that He, God, laid a siege against his attackers, the people of Moab, Ammon, and Mt. Seir.
It reads:
"And when they began to sing and praise, the LORD set ambushments against the children of Ammon, Moab, and Mount Seir, which were come against Judah; and they were smitten."

At this stage, sing at least three songs of praises to God.
Then Pray like this: The great, the mighty, and powerful God of war, thank You for the battles You undertake on our behalf. May honour, power, might, worship, adoration, and praises remain with You in Jesus' Name.

Psalm 150:6 reads:
"Let everything that hath breath, praise the LORD. Praise ye the LORD."
The blind, the lame, the dumb, the terminally sick, the pauper, the born-again, and non-born again, all praise and give thanks to You, Most Merciful Father in Heaven, may our praises and thanksgiving come into Your heart and gladden It in Jesus' name.

Psalm 29:1–2 reads:

"Give unto the LORD glory and strength. Give unto the LORD, the glory due unto his name; worship the LORD in the beauty of holiness."

Worship and thank God.

Psalm 33:2–3 reads:

"Praise the LORD with harp: sing unto him with the psaltery and instrument of ten strings. Sing unto him a new song; play skilfully with a loud noise."

We shall continue to sing unto You, Holy God, a joyful song, with different musical instruments because You are worthy to be praised in Jesus' name.

Psalm 100:1–2 reads:

"Make a joyful noise unto the LORD, all ye lands. Serve the LORD with gladness: come before His presence with singing. Know ye that the LORD he is God: it is he that hath made us, and not we ourselves; we are his people, and the sheep of his pasture."

O Holy King of Glory, we are created by You for the purpose of praising and serving You. We shall live to always fulfil this obligation in Jesus' name.

Psalm 105:1–3 reads:

"O give thanks unto the LORD; call upon his name: make known his deeds among the people. Sing unto him, sing Psalm unto him: talk ye of all his wondrous works. Glory ye in his holy name: let the heart of them rejoice that seek the LORD."

We shall seek You in holiness, O Lord, and also rejoice, exalt, and make known Your wondrous works towards us in Jesus' name.

Isaiah 49:13 reads:
"Sing, O heaven; and be joyful, O earth; and break forth into singing, O mountain: for the LORD hath comforted his people, and will have mercy upon his afflicted."
Most merciful Lord of all comforts, who has compassion on His children, may worship, praises, glory, honour be unto You forever in Jesus' name.

Psalm 150:2 reads:
"Praise him for his mighty acts: praise him according to his excellent greatness."
The great, the mighty, the powerful God, You are great and greatly to be praised. Be thou glorified forever in Jesus' name.

Psalm 107:1–2 reads:
"O give thanks unto the LORD, for he is good: for his mercy endureth forever. Let the redeemed of the LORD say so, whom he had redeemed from the hand of the enemy".
We thank You, most merciful Lord, because You have redeemed us from the hand of our enemies and for Your goodness and mercy. Be thou magnified in Jesus' name.

Psalm 113:1–3 reads:
"Praise ye the LORD. Praise, O ye servants of the LORD,

praise the name of the LORD. Blessed be the name of the LORD from this time forth and forever more. From the rising of the sun, unto the going down of the same the LORD's name is to be praised."

We shall continue to praise Your name, O Lord, forever more, for at Your name, every knee shall bow in Jesus' name.

Psalm 117:1–2 reads:

"O praise the LORD, all ye nations: praise him all ye people. For his merciful kindness is great toward us: and the truth of the LORD endureth for ever."

We praise and magnify You, O Holy Lord, even as Your kindness and truth flow toward us in Jesus' name.

Isaiah 53:4–5 reads:

"Surely he hath borne our griefs, and carried our sorrows: yet we did esteem him stricken, smitten of God, and afflicted. But he was wounded for our transgressions, he was bruised for our iniquities: the chastisement of our peace was upon him, and with his stripes we are healed."

O great and mighty Redeemer, we thank You for that deep pain You endured willingly for our salvation. Let glory, love, honour, adoration, be unto You forever and ever in the name of Jesus.

Isaiah 25:1, 4 reads:

"O LORD, thou art my God; I will exalt thee, I will praise thy name; for thou hast done wonderful things; thy counsels of old are faithfulness and truth... For thou hast been a strength to the poor, a strength to the needy in his distress, a refuge from the storm, a shadow from the heat, when the blast of the terrible ones is as a storm against the wall."

We thank and praise You, most merciful God for You are our Strength, Refuge, and Power at a time of distress and trouble. May our lives glorify You in Jesus' name.

Psalm 66:8–9 reads:

"O bless our God, ye people, and make the voice of his praise to be heard: which holdeth our soul in life, and suffereth not our feet to be moved."

We thank and bless You, O Holy God, for life, protection, and sustenance. Be thou exalted, O most righteous and powerful God in Jesus' name.

Colossians 1:12, 19–20 reads:

"Giving thanks unto the Father, which hath made us meet to be partakers of the inheritance of the saints in light. ... For it pleased the Father that in Him should all fullness dwell; and, having made peace through the blood of his cross, by him to reconcile all things unto himself."

We thank You, most loving God, for revealing the hidden mystery of ages ago to us. We thank You, most merciful Redeemer, Jesus Christ, for the agony on the cross, for the salvation of our souls. To You be praises, thanksgiving, glory, honour, dominion, worship, adoration, exaltation, service, love from Your children forever more in Jesus' name.

Matthew 8:20 reads:

"And Jesus saith unto him, 'The foxes have holes, and the birds of the air have nests; but the Son of man hath not where to lay his head.' "

Thou Lord, the Light of the world, who on this earth was made a wanderer for my sake, as You were wandering, Your heart though focused, was also wandering. We thank you for the lesson of endurance in times of affliction and deprivation. We praise and thank You for the spirit of humility and discipline. Please receive love, service, adoration, and worship from Your children in the name Jesus.

Thank God for answered prayers.

Chapter 3

HOLINESS AND RIGHTEOUSNESS

Please do the prayers on forgiveness and praises first before going into any of the prayers in this book. Prayers for holiness and righteousness are the prayers that God may answer easily because the Word of God in Matthew 6:33 reads:

"Seek ye first the kingdom of God, and his righteousness; and other things shall be added unto you." Holiness and righteousness are solid foundation on which your relationship with Christ will be based.

Matthew 12:31 reads:

"Wherefore I say unto you, all manner of sin and blasphemy shall be forgiven unto men; but the blasphemy against the Holy Ghost shall not be forgiven unto men." Everlasting Redeemer, please give me the grace to live in total obedience to the Holy Spirit in Jesus' name.

O Holy God, please let any power masquerading God, the Lord Jesus Christ, or the Holy Spirit in my life receive Your immediate attention and be uprooted in Jesus' Name.

Let any satanic agent masquerading as husband, wife, mother, children in our dreams, receive Your immediate attention and be uprooted in Jesus' Name.

Matthew 15:13 reads:
"Every plant, which my heavenly Father hath not planted, shall be rooted out."
O Holy God, please let all satanic powers in the body of Christ, which You did not plant there, be seriously dealt with in the name of Jesus.
My Holy Father and my God, please uphold the body of Christ against all spiritual attacks in Jesus' name.
O God, please let the body of Christ receive permanent spiritual deliverance in Jesus' name.

Proverbs 4:26–27 reads:
"Ponder the path of thy feet, and let all thy ways be established. Turn not to the right nor to the left: remove thy foot from evil."
Father Lord, please give me the grace to recognize and ignore satanic distractions in my life in Jesus' Name.

Psalm 5:8 reads:
"Lead me, O LORD, in thy righteousness because of mine enemies; make thy way straight before my face."
O Holy God of all righteousness, please give me the grace always to live a holy life, so that the plans of my enemies will fail forever in my life in Jesus' name.

Proverbs 8:8 reads:

"All the words of my mouth are in righteousness; there is nothing froward or perverse in them."

O God, please empower me to speak and do only what is right before Thee in Jesus' name.

Jeremiah 10:23–24 reads:

"O LORD, I know that the way of man is not in himself: it is not in man that walketh to direct his steps. O LORD, please correct me, but with judgement (mercy); not in thine anger, lest thou bring me to nothing."

Holy God, please help me to accept corrections, and be able to reject the onset of sin in my life in the name of Jesus.

James 5:16 reads:

"The effectual fervent prayer of a righteous man availeth much."

O Holy God of Truth and Mercy, please empower me to walk in the path of righteousness so that I will always experience answered prayers in Jesus' name.

Psalm 19:14 reads:

"Let the words of my mouth, and the meditation of my heart, be acceptable in thy sight, O LORD, my strength, and my Redeemer."

O God, please give me the power to resist the habit of speaking careless words and nurturing unholy thoughts in my heart, so that I can approach You in righteousness in Jesus' name.

Meditate on the picture of Christ on the cross and His holiness, for at least five minutes without thinking of any other thing. If distracted, start again.

1 Peter 2:24 reads:
"Who his own self bare our sins in his own body on the tree, that we being dead to sins, should live unto righteousness: by whose stripes ye were healed."
My Holy Father and my God, please let the nature of sin die in my life and never be resurrected again in Jesus' name. Eternal God of all righteousness, please lead me away from sin for Thy name's sake. Please let Your anointing to resist sin flow into my spirit, soul, and body, and deliver me in the name of Jesus.

Matthew 11:28–30 reads:
"Come unto me, all ye that labour and are heavy laden, and I will give you rest. Take my yoke upon you, and learn of me; for I am meek and lowly in heart: and ye shall find rest unto your souls. For my yoke is easy, and my burden is light."
O Holy Spirit, I want to 'learn of Christ'. Please pass me through your training school, so that I may obtain perfect holiness and righteousness in Jesus' name.

Matthew 15:30 reads:
"And great multitudes came unto him, having with them those that were lame, blind, dumb, maimed, and many others, and cast them down at Jesus' feet; and he healed them."

O God, please give me the grace to minister with compassion, not with hidden pride. Empower me never to turn my back towards the needy in Jesus' name.

Malachi 4:2 reads:
"But unto you that fear my name shall the Sun of righteousness arise with healing in his wings; and ye shall go forth, and grow up as calves of the stall."
This means that healing or blessing and life after death can only come through righteousness. Everlasting Father, Thou, the Giver of life and health, please give me the grace to walk in holiness, so that at Your second advent, I may be grouped with those that will receive from You in Jesus' name.
O most blessed Holy Spirit of the living God, please train me in righteousness, so that I can recognize the hidden signs of backsliding and avoid them in Jesus' name.
Holy Spirit, please open the eyes of my understanding to recognize and reject the onset of sin before it gets on to me in Jesus' name.

Exodus 20:2–3 reads:
"I am the LORD thy God, ... Thou shalt have no other gods before me."
Make the following confession: I worship the Holy Lord, my God, Him only do I desire and serve. I will have no other gods beside Him. My enemies chose satan and multiplied their sorrows. Their drink offerings of blood I will not offer because Jesus has made once and for all sacrifice of His blood for me. I will also not take the

name of satan into my lips (Psalm 16:4).

O God, please let every day of my life vindicate my faithfulness and loyalty to You in Jesus' name.

Any power masquerading God, Jesus Christ, or the blessed Holy Spirit in my life, I pass a decree today that I am not and will never be part of that arrangement and that they will surely fail in Jesus' name.

Please Holy God, deliver me and my family from the sin of ignorance in Jesus' name.

Psalm 4:4–5 reads:

"Stand in awe, and sin not … Offer the sacrifices of righteousness, and put your trust in the LORD."

My Holy Father, and my God, I base my trust on You, please empower me to be conscious of any sin that is trying to come into my life, 24 hours every day. Please lead me in the path of righteousness because of my enemies in the name of Jesus.

O God, please let my desire and hunger to learn and to know more about You spiritually overshadow the distractions of the world in my life in Jesus' name. O God, please let the blood of Jesus cleanse my thoughts, in the name of Jesus.

John 9:4 reads:

"I must work the works of him that sent me, while it is day: the night cometh, when no man can work."

Father Lord, please uproot every spirit of procrastination, wandering thoughts, and laziness from my life in Jesus' name.

O God, please give me the grace to work hard like Jesus when He was in this world in Jesus' name. According to the Word of God in Mark 1:35, He was always "rising up a great while before day, He went out, and departed into a solitary place, and there prayed."
O Holy God, please let every spirit of satanic laziness and procrastination in my life be bound, paralysed, and cast away in Jesus' name.

Hebrews 10:7 reads:
"Then said I, Lo, I come (in the volume of the book it is written of me,) to do thy will, O God."
O Holy God, please let Your will and not the will of man guide all my thinking and actions in Jesus' name.

Matthew 18:8–9 reads:
"Wherefore, if thy hand or thy foot offend thee, cut them off, and cast them from thee: it is better for thee to enter into life halt or maimed, rather than having two hands or two feet to be cast into everlasting fire. And if thine eye offend thee, pluck it out, and cast it from thee: it is better for thee to enter into life with one eye rather than having two eyes to be cast into hell fire."
O Holy God of truth, please purge me of any sin I attracted into my life through the use of my eyes, hands, and legs. I am sorry and truly repent of them. Give me the grace to be free of them at last, so that I can please You in the name of Jesus.
Any relationship that will lead me to hell, whether human or spiritual, conscious or unconscious, please Holy God

who foresees the end from the beginning, terminate it in Jesus' name.

Matthew 15:13 reads:
"But he answered and said, "Every plant, which my heavenly Father hath not planted, shall be rooted up.' "
Everlasting Redeemer, please let anything in my life working contrary to Your divine plan for me be permanently uprooted in the name of Jesus.

Proverbs 24:9 reads:
"The thought of foolishness is sin".
Most blessed Holy Spirit, please empower me to develop the right discipline that will enable me to exercise control over my thoughts in the name of Jesus. O Lord, please monitor the movement of my thoughts, and let them be channelled to Your glory in Jesus' name.

John 12:24 reads:
"Verily, verily, I say unto you, except a corn of wheat fall into the ground and die, it abideth alone: but if it die, it bringeth forth much fruit."
Immortal Redeemer, please teach me to die to self, so that I can truly relate to You and reproduce for You in the name of Jesus.

Matthew 26:24 reads
"The Son of man goeth as it is written of him: but woe unto that man by whom the Son of man is betrayed! It had been good for that man if he had not been born."

O Holy God of power and truth, please let any enemy whether spiritual or physical, that is trying or planning to lead me away, consciously or unconsciously from You, the only true God, fail permanently and receive Your immediate attention in the name of Jesus.

Psalm 94:10–11 reads:
"He that chastiseth the heathen, shall not he correct? He that teacheth man knowledge, shall not he know? The LORD knoweth the thoughts of man, that they are vanity."
Everlasting Father of all knowledge, if I am following the wrong path, please have mercy and correct me, and do not abandon me in the name of Jesus.
Re-direct me in a way that I can follow to achieve my destiny in the name of Jesus.

1 King 22:22 reads:
"And the LORD said unto him, where with? And he said, I will go forth, and I will be a lying spirit in the mouth of all his prophets. And he said, thou shalt persuade him, and prevail also: go forth, and do so."
Most Blessed Holy Spirit, my Guardian, please help me to maintain a clean heart, so that I do not provoke or tempt the Holy God and my Lord in the name of Jesus.

1 Kings 8:58
"That he may incline our hearts unto him, to walk in all his ways, and to keep his commandments, and his statutes, and his judgements, which he commanded

our fathers."

O Holy God of all righteousness, please incline my heart towards You, so that I may obey You all the days of my life in Jesus' name.

Isaiah 52:11 reads:

"Depart ye, depart ye, go ye out from thence, touch no unclean things; go ye out of the midst of her; be ye clean, that bear the vessels of the LORD."

Holy Father God, please choose thou my companions for me in Jesus' name. Order my steps according to Your words in Psalm 37:23. Let it go along with Your will in Jesus' name.

Psalm 37:37 reads:

"Mark the perfect man, and behold the upright: for the end of that man is peace."

O Holy God of peace, please train me and my family in obedience, so that we can inherit peace and happiness in the end instead of torment and sorrow in the name of Jesus.

In this next prayer, you must cry out to God with all your heart.

Proverbs 14:12 reads: "There is a way which seemeth right unto a man, but the end thereof are the ways of death."

Holy Spirit, please lead me on the path of truth. Do not let me act in ignorance only to perish in the end in the name of Jesus.

Deuteronomy 29:29 reads:

"The secret things belong unto the LORD our God: but those things which are revealed belong unto us and to our children for ever, that we may do all the words of this law."

Jehovah Rohi, the Lord our Shepherd, please do not let me be led astray by man. Please do not let me perish for what I am ignorant of; let anything that is in opposition to You in my life be exposed, corrected, and defeated permanently in the name of Jesus.

Isaiah 1:18 reads:

"Come now, and let us reason together, saith the LORD; though your sins be as scarlet, they shall be as white as snow; though they be red like crimson, they shall be as wool."

Jehovah Mekaddishkem, the Holy God our Sanctifier, please pass me through the Holy Spirit's school of righteousness, so that my righteousness shall truly shine like light to all in the mighty name of Jesus.

Ezekiel 37:5 reads:

"Thus saith the Lod GOD unto these bones; behold, I will cause breath to enter into you, and ye shall live".

O most merciful God, the Giver of life and health, please breathe into me Your breath of life, so that new power to overcome sin will come unto me and remain with me in the mighty name of Jesus.

Psalm 18:32 reads:

"It is God that girdeth me with strength, and maketh my way perfect."

O Holy Lord God, my Shepherd and my Strength, please let Your hand of guidance and protection be placed always on me, so that I do not go astray in the mighty name of Jesus.

Psalm 19:12–13 reads:

"Who can understand his error? Cleanse thou me from secret fault. Keep back thy servant also from presumptuous sins; let them not have dominion over me: then shall I be upright, and I shall be innocent from the great transgression."

Father Lord, You are the Great God of peace. Please teach me to understand how secret and unconscious sins enter into human hearts in the mighty name of Jesus.

Eternal God of my righteousness, please give me the feeling of alertness towards any root of sin, and the power to fight it off in Jesus' name. Let the urge not to commit any sin greatly overcome the one to commit it in my life in the name of Jesus.

Jeremiah 21:14 reads:

"But I will punish you according to the fruit of your doings".

My Holy Father and my God, please give me the grace to live according to all the requirements of the fruits of the Spirit, so that I can avoid eternal punishment in the name of Jesus.

Where I fail, please correct me in Your own way, and pick me up again; but do not abandon me altogether in the name of Jesus.

Psalm 19:14 reads:
"Let the words of my mouth, and the meditation of my heart, be acceptable in thy sight, O LORD, my Strength, and my Redeemer."
Holy Spirit, please lead me into the right way of praying, so that my presentation can be acceptable before God in Jesus' name.

Jeremiah 22:13 reads:
"Woe unto him that buildeth his house by unrighteousness, and his chambers by wrong".
Eternal Rock of Ages, please do not let me labour righteously in this world only to perish in the end in the name of Jesus.

Matthew 7:26–27 reads:
"And every one that heareth these sayings of mine, and doeth them not, shall be likened unto a foolish man, which built his house upon the sand: and the rain descended, and the floods came, and the winds blew, and beat upon that house; and it fell: and great was that fall of it."
Thou Holy God, my Buckler, and the Horn of my salvation, please let anything that will make me to disobey Your word be put away from my life in the name of Jesus.

Father Lord, please do not let me be like one who came to this world to render fruitless service, and dig my own grave (God forbid) in Jesus' name.

Please Lord, hasten to put me on the right step in the name of Jesus.

Jeremiah 23:1 reads:

"Woe unto the pastors that destroy and scatter the sheep of my pasture! saith the LORD."

O God, I refuse to be misled into hell-fire by the spiritual and physical masquerades in the body of Christ. Please protect me from them in the name of Jesus.

Jeremiah 22:16 reads:

"He judged the cause of the poor and the needy; then it was well with him: was not this to know me? saith the LORD. But thine eyes and thine heart are not but for covetousness".

Holy Spirit, please lead me away from selfish thoughts and actions in the name of Jesus.

Holy God, please do not let the spirit of selfishness come into my life in the name of Jesus.

Father Lord, please give me the grace to love my neighbour as myself in Jesus' name.

Ephesians 6:14 reads:

"Stand therefore, having your loins girt about with truth, and having on the breast plate of righteousness".

O Holy God, please give me the grace to always live this

life in truth and guided by the Holy Spirit in the name of Jesus.

Ephesians 6:17 reads:
"And take the helmet of salvation, and the sword of the Spirit, which is the word of God".
Please Holy God, grant me the grace to avoid unconsciously making mockery of my salvation and the word of life in the name of Jesus.

In John 3:5 Jesus answered:
"Verily, verily, I say unto thee, except a man be born of water and of the Spirit, he cannot enter into the kingdom of God."
Everlasting Redeemer, please save me from the common sin of setting my own methods or standards of being born again in the name of Jesus. Give me the wisdom to live according to Your own requirements in the mighty name of Jesus.
O Holy God, let anything that will make me to be a stranger to the Holy Spirit be permanently uprooted from my life in the name of Jesus.

John 3:18 reads:
"He that believeth in him is not condemned: but he that believeth not is condemned already, because he hath not believed in the name of the only begotten Son of God."
Father Lord, please forgive my doubts, and as Your disciples asked You to increase their faith, please do the same to my faith in the name of Jesus.

I believe and try to order my life according to Your word. O Holy God, please help me to use Your word to resist the evil desires of the flesh in the name of Jesus.

O God, please enable me to develop the grace of being truly born again in Jesus' name.

2 Corinthians 7:2 reads:

"Receive us; we have wronged no man, we have corrupted no man, we have defrauded no man."

O God, please empower me to cleanse myself of all filthiness of the flesh and soul and to perfect holiness, so that I may be found guiltless before You in Jesus' name.

Ephesians 4:29 reads:

"Let no corrupt communication proceed out of your mouth, but that which is good to the use of edifying, that it may minister grace unto the hearers."

Holy Spirit of the living God, please help me to bind every evil and negative pronouncement, and to cast them away from my tongue in the name of Jesus.

Ephesians 4:26 reads:

"Be ye angry, and sin not: let not the sun go down upon your wrath".

Father Lord, You are the Strength of my life, I shall not fear. Please empower me to pursue, overtake, subdue, and destroy permanently the demon of fear and anger, so that it will never arise again in my life in the name of Jesus.

Romans 6:16 reads:

"Know ye not, that to whom ye yield yourselves servants to obey, his servant ye are to whom ye obey; whether of sin unto death, or of obedience unto righteousness?"

O Holy God of signs, miracles, and wonders, Your Word tells me that with You, nothing shall be impossible (Luke 1:37). Please anoint me with the anointing to hate and resist sin perfectly in the mighty name of Jesus.

Father God, please let no spirit of sin programmed against me ever prosper in the name of Jesus.

O God, please give me the spirit of alertness that will make it possible for me to be conscious of sin twenty-four hours every day in the mighty name of Jesus.

Psalm 119:40 reads:

"Behold, I have longed after thy precepts: (please) quicken me in thy righteousness."

Merciful Father of all righteousness, do not let my hunger for righteousness be unfulfilled and in vain in Jesus' name.

Matthew 4:4 reads:

"It is written, Man shall not live by bread alone, but by every word that proceedeth out of the mouth of God."

O God, my Strength and in whom I trust, please let a healthy appetite for Your Word replace the incessant appetite for food in my life in Jesus' name.

Proverbs 12:7 reads:

"The wicked are overthrown, and are not: but the house

of the righteous shall stand."

O God, please do not let me exit from this world with the guilt that I am the one responsible for my family not making heaven in Jesus' name.

Proverbs 12:14 reads:

"A man shall be satisfied with good by the fruit of his mouth: and the recompense of a man's hand shall be rendered unto him."

Father God, please do not let me build and another inhabit, do not let me plant and another reap, and do not let me labour in vain in the mighty name of Jesus.

Proverbs 25:21–22 reads:

"If thine enemy be hungry, give him bread to eat; and if he be thirsty, give him water to drink. For thou shalt heap coals of fire upon his head, and the LORD shall reward thee."

Immortal Redeemer, please enable me to develop the right attitude towards my enemies in the name of Jesus. Give me the grace to have sympathy and not hatred for them, so that I can have a right attitude towards them in Jesus' name.

Proverbs 29:7 reads

"The righteous considereth the cause of the poor: but the wicked regardeth not to know it."

Father Lord, please make me to be my brother's keeper in the mighty name of Jesus.

2 Corinthians 1:12 reads:

"For our rejoicing is this, the testimony of our conscience, that in simplicity and godly sincerity, not with fleshly wisdom, but by the grace of God, we have had our conversation in this world, and more abundantly to you-ward."

O God of all righteousness, please give me the grace to be completely yielded to You in humility and truth in the name of Jesus.

Matthew 7:21 reads:

"Not everyone that saith unto me, Lord, Lord, shall enter into the kingdom of heaven; but he that doeth the will of my Father which is in heaven."

Holy Spirit, please lead me in the way of obedience to the Word of God, so that I can abide in His grace in the name of Jesus.

Proverbs 24:9 reads:

"The thought of foolishness is sin: and the scorner is an abomination to men."

O God, please train me to nurture only healthy thoughts in my mind, and to deal with people in a respectful manner in the name of Jesus.

James 4:7 reads:

"Submit yourselves therefore to God. Resist the devil, and he will flee from you."

O God of my strength, please empower me to sustain a state of continuous submission to You always. Please release on me the anointing of a greater resistant force against sin and the devil in the name of Jesus.

John 10:5 reads:
"And a stranger will they not follow, but will flee from him: for they know not the voice of strangers."
Father Lord, please give me the grace to recognise Your voice always in Jesus' name.

Psalm 34:13–14 reads:
"Keep thy tongue from evil, and thy lips from speaking guile. Depart from evil, and do good; seek peace, and pursue it."
O Holy God of might and power, please give me the enabling grace to always keep my mouth free of all evil pronouncements, my life free from sin, and to live in peace with everybody, so that I can attain eternal life in the name of Jesus.

James 1:17 reads:
"Every good gift and every perfect gift is from above, and cometh down from the Father of lights".
O Holy God, from whom all good gifts are sent, please perfect Your grace of holiness and righteousness in me, so that I can always receive every good gift from You in the name of Jesus. Please let the attempts of the enemy to bring sin into my life always fail in Jesus' name.

James 4:17 reads:
"Therefore to him that knoweth to do good, and doeth it

not, to him it is sin."
Holy God of goodness and mercy, please as Your acts of goodness overshadow me, let my own goodness reach out and overshadow others in the name of Jesus.
Blessed Holy Spirit, please teach me to think good and not evil of my enemies in the name of Jesus.

Hebrews 11:6 reads:
"But without faith it is impossible to please him (God)".
Anytime in my life I had acted without faith or fearfully, Holy God, please forgive me in Jesus' name.
May the spirit of living in fear die permanently in my life in Jesus' name.

2 Peter 1:4 reads:
"Whereby are given unto us exceeding great and precious promise: that by these ye might be partakers of the divine nature, having escaped the corruption that is in the world through lust."
Everlasting Father, please empower me to mortify my flesh, so that I shall not be subject to the sins of lust of the flesh, the eyes, the appetite, and the mouth in the name of Jesus.
O Holy God of truth, please let anything that will ensnare me to sin and also render me ignorant of its consequences not be found in my life in the name of Jesus.

Isaiah 1:19–20 reads:
"If ye are willing and obedient, ye shall eat the good of the land: but if ye refuse and rebel, ye shall be devoured

with the sword: for the mouth of the LORD hath spoken it."

O God, please give me a willing spirit that will enable me to obey the Word and to be found worthy of the fruits of the land in Jesus' name.

2 Peter 1:6 reads:

"And to knowledge temperance; and to temperance patience; and to patience goodliness".

My Holy Father and my God, please give me the enabling grace to always deal with my fellow human beings in a disciplined and tolerant manner in the name of Jesus.

2 Peter 2:8 reads:

"For that righteous man dwelling among them, in seeing and hearing, vexed his righteous soul from day to day with their unlawful deeds".

Immortal Redeemer, please do not let me be ensnared into sin by the manipulations, temptations, masquerading, and attacks of Satan operating around me and in my dreams in the name of Jesus. Give me the wisdom, knowledge, and understanding of Your Word in order to be able to overcome, and to help others to do so in the name of Jesus.

Hebrews 5:8 reads:

"Though he were a Son, yet learned he obedience by the things which he suffered".

Eternal King of glory, the Creator of knowledge, please let me learn perfect obedience to You by the suffering I am passing through. May the suffering not be a waste in my life in Jesus' name.

2 Peter 2:21 reads:
"For it had been better for them not to have known the way of righteousness, than, after they have known it, to turn from the holy commandment delivered unto them."
God of mercy, please shield me under Thy wings, and do not allow one moment of pleasure and satanic relief lure me away into the camp of hell fire in the name of Jesus.

Hebrews 6:12 reads:
"That ye be not slothful, but followers of them who through faith and patience inherit the promises."
Father God, after running this race to meet You, please do not let over confidence and idleness creep into my life and cost me Your reward in the name of Jesus.

Hebrews 12:22–23 reads:
"But ye are come unto mount Zion, and unto the city of the living God, the heavenly Jerusalem, and to an innumerable company of angels, to the general assembly and church of the firstborn, which are written in heaven, and to God the Judge of all, and to the spirits of just men made perfect".
O Holy God to whom salvation, glory, power, and honour belongs, please empower me to live in a way that will make it possible for You to perfect my spirit, soul, and body for heavenly abode in Jesus' name.

Hebrews 6:1 reads:

"Therefore leaving the principles of the doctrine of Christ, let us go on to perfection".

O Holy God of power and might, please move me forward with your fire. Let the spirit of backwardness and stagnation depart completely from my spiritual life in the name of Jesus.

Psalm 51:17 reads:

"The sacrifices of God are a broken spirit: a broken and a contrite heart, O God, thou wilt not despise."

O Holy Lord, by Your power, please break me down completely, and mould me for your purposes in the name of Jesus. O God, let Your will be made perfect in my life in the name of Jesus.

Romans 14:17–18 reads:

"For the kingdom of God is not meat and drink; but righteousness, and peace, and joy in the Holy Ghost. For he that in these things serveth Christ is acceptable to GOD, and approved of men."

Father Lord, please empower me to serve You in holiness, righteousness, and peace, to the exclusion of every other distraction, so that in the end, I may rejoice with You in Heaven in Jesus name.

John 3:5 reads:

"Jesus answered, "Verily, verily, I say unto thee, except a man be born of water and of the Spirit, he cannot enter into the kingdom of God."

Eternal Redeemer, please forgive me if I have set my own standards and requirements for entering heaven. Please enable me to fulfil Your own requirements in John 3:5 and also as explained by Jesus in the Beatitudes in the name of Jesus.

1 Corinthians 2:9 reads:
"But as it is written, eye hath not seen, nor ear heard, neither have entered into the heart of man, the things which God hath prepared for them that love him."
Holy God of comfort, please, out of Your mercy, help me to be very receptive to the word of God and to obey it all, so that I shall qualify for the blessing You prepared for them that love You in the name of Jesus.

James 1:22 reads:
"But be ye doers of the word, and not hearers only, deceiving your own selves."
O God, please give me the grace to live the Word that I read and speak in the mighty name of Jesus.

1 Sam 15:22a, 23b reads:
"Hath the Lord as great delight in burnt offering and sacrifices, as in obeying the voice of the Lord? ... Because thou hast rejected the word of the Lord, he hath also rejected thee from being king."
O God, please enable me to always remember that the rejection of and disobedience to Your word will lead to condemnation in the name of Jesus.

Romans 9:15 reads:

"For he saith to Moses, I will have mercy on whom I will have mercy, and I will have compassion on whom I will have compassion."

Luke 1:50 reads:

"And his mercy is on them that fear him from generation to generation."

O Thou most merciful and long-suffering God, please give me the grace to appreciate You more and more. Do not withdraw Your mercies from me in the name of Jesus.

Isaiah 40:31 reads:

"But they that wait upon the Lord shall renew their strength; they shall mount up with wings as eagles; they shall run, and not be weary; and they shall walk, and not faint."

O Holy God, my eternal Energizer, please renew my strength day by day as I wait on You, so that I shall not faint in the name of Jesus.

Psalm 27:1b reads

"The LORD is the Strength of my life; of whom shall I be afraid?"

Thou Holy God, the Strength of my salvation, I depend on You, please uphold me in Your strength and power until the end of my journey, so that I shall neither fear, nor derail in Jesus' name.

Isaiah 61:11 reads:

"For as the earth bringeth forth her bud, and as the garden causeth the things that are sown in it to spring forth; so the Lord GOD will cause righteousness and praise to spring forth before all the nations."

O God of righteousness and power, please let our righteousness and praise for You overshadow our lives, and let us also reproduce the same for You in Jesus' name.

Romans 8:2 reads:

"For the law of the Spirit of life in Christ Jesus hath made me free from the law of sin and death."

O Holy GOD of eternal life, please by Thy power, break every yoke of sin in my life, and empower me to live the kingdom life in my heart, and to attain eternal life in Jesus' name.

Philippians 4:8 reads:

"Finally, brethren, whatsoever things are true, whatsoever things are honest, whatsoever things are just, whatsoever things are pure, whatsoever things are lovely, whatsoever things are of good report; if there be any virtue, and if there be any praise, think on these things."

O GOD, by Your name and by Your power, please create in me a clean heart, and purge my thoughts with the blood of Jesus, so that I can only think right and speak good in the name of Jesus.

Isaiah 33:15–16 reads:

"He that walketh righteously, and speaketh uprightly;

he that despiseth the gain of oppressions, that shaketh his hands from holding of bribes, that stoppeth his ears from hearing of blood, and shutteth his eyes from seeing evil; he shall dwell on high: his place of defence shall be the munitions of rocks: bread shall be given him; his waters shall be sure."

O Holy Lord, by Your power and by Your mercy, please teach me to live a sinless, honest life, so that all these rewards will be mine in Jesus' name.

Proverbs 14:12 reads:

"There is a way which seemeth right unto a man, but the end thereof are the ways of death."

Everlasting Father, please teach me to be submissive to Your Word and the instructions of the Holy Spirit, so that I do not perish in Jesus' name.

2 Sam 12:13 reads:

"And David said unto Nathan, I have sinned against the LORD. And Nathan said unto David, the LORD also hath put away thy sin, thou shalt not die."

Most merciful and forgiving Father, please help me not to be ashamed to confess the sins which I was not ashamed to commit in Jesus' name.

Help me always to empty my heart of all sins in the name of Jesus.

2 Peter 1:5–7 reads:

"And beside this, giving all diligence, add to your faith virtue; and to virtue knowledge; and to knowledge temperance; and to temperance patience; and to patience godliness; and to godliness brotherly kindness; and to brotherly kindness charity."

O Holy God of perfection, please let spiritual and moral excellence be the pattern of my life in Jesus' name.

Proverbs 18:10 reads:

"The name of the LORD is a strong tower: the righteous runneth into it, and is safe."

O Thou the Strong Tower of my life, I run into You with my family; please save us from the daily attacks and defilement by our spiritual and physical enemies. Let us not be ashamed in Jesus' name.

If you do not remember to pray other prayers, please do not ever forget this prayer against backsliding. It is a great weapon against Satan's last card in the lives of the children of God. Many servants of God of this age have suddenly fallen back to sin because they forgot the seriousness of this type of prayer.

Many people in the Bible were pulled down; those who recovered had the mercy of God. People like Abiram, Dathan, Korah and their families, Samson, Saul, Gideon, the prophet from Judah, Ananias and Saphira, perished because of the very sin of backsliding.

2 Peter 2:20 reads:

"For if after they escaped the pollutions of the world through the knowledge of the Lord and Saviour Jesus Christ, they are again entangled therein, and are overcome, the latter end is worse with them than the beginning."

Jehovah Nissi, our Banner, by Your mercies, O Holy God, please empower me not to relinquish the grounds that I have already gained in holiness and righteousness in Jesus' name.

Please give me the grace to recognize, fight, and resist the move of Satan to initiate backsliding in my life in the name of Jesus.

Isaiah 55:7 reads:

"Let the wicked forsake his way, and the unrighteous man his thoughts: and let him return unto the LORD, and he will have mercy upon him; and to God for he will abundantly pardon."

Most of these prayers are based on grace which operates the new covenant of repentance and remission of sins. For the covenant to work, the two parties have to be in agreement. Where one party refuses, for example, to repent, the covenant will not stand. The individual is abandoned to the judgment of GOD.

O Holy GOD of war, please let that enemy of my father's house, who is determined to draw me away from repentance and from Christ, receive Your immediate attention and fail permanently in the name of Jesus.

O GOD, please let any power that has refused to accept the reality of the Blood of Jesus in my life be disgraced, defeated, and uprooted permanently from my life in the name of Jesus.

1 Corinthians 10:13 reads:

"There hath no temptation taken you but such as is

common to man: but God is faithful, who will not suffer you to be tempted above that ye are able; but will with the temptation make a way to escape, that ye may be able to bear it."

O Holy GOD, please give me the power to overcome all temptations that will arise. Let me not be a negative exception in the name of Jesus.

Romans 9:8 reads:

"That is, they which are the children of the flesh, these are not the children of God: but the children of the promise are counted for the seed."

O Holy GOD of righteousness, the Eternal Foundation of Holiness, please do not allow anything of the flesh to be found in me in Jesus' name. Let me be counted among the children of the Seed in the name of Jesus.

Romans 9:15–16 reads:

"For he saith to Moses, I will have mercy on whom I will have mercy, and I will have compassion on whom I will have compassion. So then it is not of him that willeth, nor of him that runneth, but of God that showeth mercy."

Our Most Heavenly Father, perfect in mercy and everlasting kindness, please bring me to the full realization of the fact that it is only by Your mercy that I can achieve anything that is worthwhile in this world and beyond in Jesus' name.

Romans 9:27–28 reads:

"Though the number of the children of Israel be as the

sand of the sea, a remnant shall be saved: for he will finish the work, and cut it short in righteousness: because a short work will the Lord make upon the earth."

O Holy GOD of holiness and perfection, please do not exclude me and my family from Your work of righteousness in the name of Jesus.

1 Peter 5:10 reads:

"But the God of all grace, who hath called us to his eternal glory by Christ Jesus, after that ye have suffered a while, make you perfect, stablish, strengthen, settle you."

O most merciful and loving GOD, please may my labours and sufferings in this world not go without encouragement and reward in Jesus' name. Please keep me away from mistakes in Jesus' name.

Galatians 6:7–8 reads:

"Be not deceived; God is not mocked: for whatsoever a man soweth, that shall he also reap. For he that soweth to his flesh shall of the flesh reap corruption; but he that soweth to the Spirit shall of the Spirit reap life everlasting."

Holy Father God, please minister to the enemies, who are sowing evil seeds in my life, a genuine spirit of repentance, so that they do not perish in their wickedness in Jesus' name. Please also minister to me the spirit of forgiveness towards them in the name of Jesus.

Acts 1:8 reads:

"But ye shall receive power, after that the Holy Ghost is come upon you: and ye shall be witnesses unto me both in Jerusalem, and in all Judah, and in Samaria, and unto the uttermost part of the earth."

O Holy GOD of our salvation, please give me the power and the resources that will make it possible for me to carry the gospel to the farthest parts of the world in the name of Jesus.

Let me fight to win all souls for You in the name of Jesus.

Matthew 18:21–22 reads:

"Then came Peter to him, and said, Lord, how oft shall my brother sin against me and I forgive him, seven times? Jesus saith unto him, "I say not unto thee, until seven times: but until seventy times seven."

Everlasting Father, merciful, forgiving, and loving, please give me the grace to continue in the spirit of forgiveness without minding the number of times I forgive in Jesus' name.

Holy Spirit, please impart in me a genuine spirit of love for my enemies in Jesus' name.

Genesis 1:31 reads

"And God saw everything that He had made, and behold, it was very good. And the evening and the morning were the sixth day."

O Holy GOD of goodness, because I worship you, I claim the goodness of everyday that You created. I reject all the evil that Satan will plant any day in the name of Jesus.

John 14:20 reads:

"At that day ye shall know that I am in my Father, and ye

in me, and I in you."

Everlasting Redeemer, please give me the grace to live in a union of one mind and purpose with You always and with my brethren in the name of Jesus. Let every eye that sees me also perceive You in me in the name of Jesus.

1 Corinthians 2:9 reads:

"But as it is written, eye hath not seen, nor ear heard, neither have entered into the heart of man, the things which God hath prepared for them that love him."

O God, the Eternal Rewarder of righteousness, please empower me to overlook the afflictions of this world, and be encouraged by the future blessings of the Kingdom in the name of Jesus.

Matthew 16:23 reads:

"But He turned and said unto Peter, 'Get thee behind me Satan: thou art an offence unto me: for thou savourest not the things that be of God, but those that be of men. … If any man will come after me, let him deny himself and take up his cross and follow me.' "

Most blessed Holy Spirit of the living God, please use Your power to guide me away from the things of the flesh; the very things that swallow people's salvation in the mighty name of Jesus.

Help me to come to terms with the afflictions of this world knowing that my Redeemer will deliver me from them all. Let no bone of mine be broken in the name of Jesus.

Daniel 2:22 reads:

"He revealeth the deep and secret things: he knoweth what is in the darkness, and the light dwelleth with him."

Please Holy GOD, reveal to me that weak point in my character that is holding me back from achieving true righteousness and holiness, and from walking in line with my destiny in the name of Jesus.

Thank You, Lord, in Jesus' name.

Just accept the revelation with gratefulness. Any argument will only aggravate your situation.

Revelation 4:11 reads:

"Thou art Worthy, O Lord, to receive glory and honour and power".

O Holy GOD, please do not allow me to steal Your glory in ignorance. Please reveal to me any onset of this unfortunate habit, so that I can avoid it in the name of Jesus.

Gal 5:22–23 reads:

"But the Fruit of the Spirit is love, joy, peace, longsuffering, gentleness, goodness, faith, meekness, temperance: against such there is no law."

O Holy GOD, please give me the grace to live always according to all the fruits of the Spirit in Jesus' name. Please pass me through the spiritual training school of the Holy Spirit successfully in Jesus' name.

Psalm 37:31 reads:

"The law of his God is in his heart; none of his steps shall slide."

O God, please help me to retain Your word in my heart and to practice it, so that I do not slide back into sin again in Jesus' name.

1 Timothy 4:10 reads:

"For therefore we both labour and suffer reproach, because we trust in the living God, who is the Saviour of all men, specially of those that believe."

O Most Holy God, please empower me to sustain my faith in You, so that I can endure all the tribulations of this world in Jesus' name.

John 15:2 reads:

"Every branch in me that beareth not fruit he taketh away: and every branch that beareth fruit, he purgeth it, that it may bring forth more fruit."

O Lord, my High Priest and Judge, please give me the grace to be well purged by God the Father, so that I will bear good fruit and serve Him better in Jesus' name.

John 14:31 reads:

"But that the world may know that I love the Father; and as the Father gave me commandment, even so I do."

O God, my Shepherd, who leads me into obedience, please empower me to abide obediently in Your service as a manifestation of my love for You in Jesus' name.

Leviticus 11:45b reads:

"Ye shall therefore be holy, for I am holy."

O Holy God, please help me to be occupied twenty-four hours a day with the thought of trying to detect and resist any on-coming sin into my life. Keep me on the path of holiness in Jesus' name.

John 14:26 reads:
"But the Comforter, which is the Holy Ghost, whom the Father will send in my name, he shall teach you all things, and bring all things to your remembrance, whatsoever I have said unto you."
O God, please give me the grace to abide obediently under the training and guidance of the Holy Spirit, so that I can learn and remember all things pertaining to Christ and the Kingdom in Jesus' name.

1 John 3:8 reads:
"He that committeth sin is of the devil; for the devil sinneth from the beginning."
O God of all truth, please give me the power to be preoccupied, twenty-four hours every day with the consciousness of any oncoming sin, and how to avert it in Jesus' name.
Holy Father God, please give me the grace not to stray into the territory of Satan through ignorance in Jesus' name.

Hebrews 12:14
"Follow peace with all men, and holiness, without which no man shall see the Lord."
O Holy God of all righteousness, please empower me to

perceive in endurance in my relationship with my fellow human beings, so that I am not found wanting in the end in the name of Jesus.

Hebrews 12:15
"Looking diligently lest any man fail of the grace of God; lest any root of bitterness springing up trouble you, and thereby many be defiled".
O God, the Strength of my life, please give me the power to recognise the attempt of the enemy to deceive and to lead me astray from Your path, and empower me to resist this successfully in Jesus' name.

Hebrews 13:16
"But to do good and to communicate forget not: for with such sacrifices God is well pleased."
O God, please bestow on me the right spirit to be able to share my knowledge of the word of God with my neighbours in Jesus' name.
End this section with the following confessional prayers:
Spirit of sin, I bind you, and cast you away in Jesus' name.
Spirit of ignorance, I bind you, and cast you away in Jesus' name.
Spirit of forgetfulness, I bind you, and cast you away in Jesus' name.
Spirit of backsliding, I bind you, and cast you away in the name of Jesus.
I refuse to enter into the trap of satan in Jesus' name.
I plead the blood of Jesus on these prayers in Jesus' name.

Holy Spirit, please quicken my righteousness in Jesus' name.

Chapter 4

HEALING

General

Healing is in God's plan of redemption for mankind. The scripture in Exodus 15:26 states that "I am the LORD that healeth thee."

God is the one who authorized that healing; the one whom the doctors return you to when they can no longer prove the success of drugs on you. He is the Inventor of modern medicine, the Enabler of doctors, the King and Creator of physicians. He operates His own spiritual surgical theatre. He is the one who has the knowledge of how to put right those organs of your body which He created. This is because He created you, and can tell what is wrong with your organs at a glance; He even knows the number of the hair on your head. Math.10:30

Sometimes, after healing has been released, it may still take some time before the effect is felt by the sick. This is where faith and its exercise comes in. When Hezekiah received direct healing from God, he had to wait for 3 days before the effect of the healing materialized. When Abraham and Sarah's blessings were promised, it took many years before it came to pass. Every blessing goes with appropriat faith in God.

If you come to God for healing and your spiritual life is not right, He may first try to heal the spiritual before the physical.

In Exodus 15:26, we have the covenant of healing which is very explicit on the emphasis on obedience before receiving healing. It reads:

"And said, if thou wilt diligently hearken to the voice of the LORD thy God, and wilt do that which is right in his sight, and wilt give ear to his commandments, and keep all his statutes, I will put none of these diseases upon thee, which I have brought upon the Egyptians: for I am the Lord that healeth thee." When you talk of obedience, faith is paramount.

If you are asking to be healed so that you can go and make more money in order to spend it on your pleasure, please be warned that such a request may not be answered. If you are asking to be healed so that you can continue on the work of God, your petition is not selfishly motivated but based on the will of God for your life.

PRAYERS:
John 11:43–44 reads:
"And when he thus had spoken he cried with a loud voice, Lazarus come forth. And he loosed him and let

him go".

As Lazarus who had been dead for 4 days was resurrected, please Holy God, Jehovah Rapha, let my good health which the enemy has bound these years, be loosed and resurrected, in the name of Jesus.

Luke 7:13–15 reads:

"And when the Lord saw her, he had compassion on her, and said unto her, Weep not. And he came and touched the bier: and they that bare him stood still. And he said, Young man, I say unto thee, Arise. And he that was dead sat up, and began to speak. And he delivered him to his mother."

O Holy Lord of compassion, please let these sick organs in my body that seem dead these years, be now commanded to come to life again and be used for Your service in Jesus' name.

Ezekiel 37:4–6 reads:

"Again he said unto me, Prophesy upon these bones, and say unto them, O ye dry bones hear the word of the LORD. Thus saith the LORD God unto these bones; Behold, I will cause breath to enter into you, and ye shall live: And I will lay sinews upon you, and will bring up flesh upon you, and cover you with skin, and put breath in you, and ye shall live, and ye shall know that I am the LORD."

O Holy God of miracles, signs, and wonders, I stand on Your word in Ezekiel 37:4–6 above and on Mark 11:24

which says, "What thing so ever ye desire, when ye pray, believe that ye receive them, and ye shall have them." I pray that the same power that made the dry bones to be alive again, and the faith which You talked about in Mark 11:24, which I am currently exercising, will renew the life of these my bones that have been troubled over the years by in Jesus' name.

Proverbs 10:27 reads:
"The fear of the LORD prolongeth days: but the years of the wicked shall be shortened."
O Holy Father of life and health, please put the right fear of You inside me, so that my years will not be shortened. Empower me always to maintain that fear for the rest of my life, in Jesus' name.

Matthew 8:8, 10, 13 reads:
"The centurion answered and said, Lord, I am not worthy that thou shouldest come under my roof: but speak the word only, and my servant shall be healed. …
 "When Jesus heard it, he marvelled, and said to them that followed, Verily I say unto you, I have not found so great faith, no, not in Israel. …
"And Jesus said unto the centurion, Go thy way; and as thou hast believed, so be it done unto thee. And his servant was healed in the selfsame hour."
O Jehovah Rapha, the great Healer, though my eyes do not see You, though this infirmity/sickness has advanced for many years, yet by my faith and the miracles that You do, I do believe that You are perfectly able to heal me

now. Please uphold this faith that I have, and heal me of this sickness, so that the world will believe and glorify You, Father, again and again for what You are in Jesus' name.

Jeremiah 30:17 reads:
"For I will restore health unto thee, and I will heal thee of thy wounds, saith the LORD".
O Holy God of life and health, please speak health and life unto this body again in Jesus' name.

Deuteronomy 7–15 reads:
"And the LORD shall take away from thee all sickness, and will put none of the evil diseases of Egypt, which thou knowest, upon thee; but will lay them upon all them that hate thee."
Father Lord, I seek to do Your will. Please do not let sickness, diseases, and infirmity be my lot or hinder me, in Jesus' name.

Jeremiah. 17:14 reads:
"Heal me, O Lord, and I shall be healed; save me and I shall be saved: for thou art my praise."
O Lord God, please heal me of all sicknesses, diseases etc. Let my healing glorify You in the name of Jesus.

Acts 3:16 reads:
"And his name through faith in his name hath made this man strong, whom ye see and know: yea, the faith which is by him hath given him this perfect soundness in the

presence of you all."

Shout the name of Jesus seven times. Pray: O God of my salvation, please let the power in the name of Jesus, the name at which every knee must bow, set me free from this sickness, infirmity, in the name of Jesus. Fill in the gap.

3 John 1:2 reads:
"Beloved I wish above all things that thou mayest prosper and be in health, even as thy soul prospereth."
Pray: O Thou great Physician, please let my divine health and prosperity materialize now and glorify You even as my soul prospers in the name of Jesus. Father Lord, please heal me, so that my health and my soul will glorify You in Jesus' name. Please remove all hindrances to my recovery and let me live to declare and do Your work in the land of the living, in Jesus' name.

Exodus 15:26 reads:
"And said, If thou wilt diligently hearken to the voice of the LORD thy God, and wilt do that which is right in his sight, and wilt give ear to His Commandments, and keep all his statutes, I will put none of these diseases upon thee, which I have brought upon the Egyptians; for I am the LORD that healeth thee."
O God, please let anything that will continue to bring sin, disobedience, and sickness into my life be uprooted from my life forever in Jesus' name.

Psalm 34 19–20 reads:

"Many are the afflictions of the righteous: but the LORD delivereth him out of them all. He keepeth all his bones: not one of them is broken."

Jehovah Rapha, my great Healer, please heal all my sickness, diseases, and infirmity, and restore me back to my state of perfect heath, in Jesus' name.

Psalm 107:20 reads:

"He sent his word, and healed them, and delivered them from their destructions."

Holy Father God, my great Physician, please let Your word perform its healing powers in my body, and deliver me from all my afflictions in Jesus' name.

Isaiah 53:5 reads:

"But he was wounded for our transgressions, He was bruised for our iniquities; the chastisement for our peace was upon him, and with his stripes we are healed."

In the name of Jesus, I stand by faith on this word of God and claim healing for my … Repeat several times: "I claim healing for my … in the name of Jesus. (Fill in the gap).

Jeremiah 17:14 reads:

"Heal me, O LORD, and I shall be healed: save me, and I shall be saved: for thou art my praise."

Repeat this quotation several times with faith inserting the name of your particular sickness and add 'in Jesus' name.

Jeremiah 33:6 reads:

"Behold, I will bring it health and cure, and I will cure them, and will reveal unto them the abundance of peace and truth."

Let Thy healing power, O God, restore back health and peace to me, so that I can serve You well, in Jesus' name.

Joel 3:21 reads:

"For I will cleanse their blood that I have not cleansed".

O Thou most merciful God, the true Physician, please use the blood of Jesus to cleanse my blood, in Jesus' name. O let the blood of Jesus flow into my spirit, soul, and body, in Jesus' name. Repeat this second prayer several times over.

Malachi 4: 2

"But unto you that fear my name shall the Sun of righteousness arise with healing in his wings; and ye shall go forth and grow up as calves of the stall."

Holy Spirit, please help me to live a righteous life inside and outside, so that I may always receive divine healing from the Lord in Jesus' name.

John 8:36 reads:

"If the Son therefore shall make you free, ye shall be free indeed."

O God of power and deliverance, please let Your right hand of mercy and deliverance set me free from my spiritual and physical foundational enemies in Jesus' name.

Isaiah 58:6–8 reads:

"Is not this the fast that I have chosen? to loose the bands of wickedness, to undo the heavy burdens, and to let the oppressed go free, and that ye break every yoke? Is it not to deal thy bread to the hungry, and that thou bring the poor that are cast out to thy house? when thou seest the naked, that thou cover him; and that thou hide not thyself from thine own flesh? Then shall thy light break forth as the morning".

As I fast and pray, O Holy Lord, please teach and empower me to do so in the right way, so that I do not labour and waste my time in vain in Jesus' name. You have to pray this last prayer with a fast in the context of Isaiah 58:6–7.

2 Kings 20:5 reads:

"Thus saith the LORD, the God of David thy father, I have heard thy prayer, I have seen thy tears: behold I will heal thee".

Jehovah Rapha, my great Healer, please have mercy on me in the name of Jesus. Behold my tears which have not ceased to flow, behold my prayers that I render to you every day, forgive my sins that are standing between You and me. I truly repent of them; please heal me now in Jesus' name.

Psalm 67:2 reads:

"That thy way may be known upon earth, thy saving health among all nations."

Heal me, O most merciful God, so that You will be glorified on earth, and many souls won for You in Jesus' name.

Psalm 41:3 reads:
"The LORD will strengthen him upon the bed of languishing: thou wilt make all his bed in his sickness."
Thou great Physician, Jehovah Rapha, please minister healing to my spirit, soul, and body in the name of Jesus.

Hosea 13:14 reads:
"I will ransom them from the power of the grave; I will redeem them from death; O death, I will be thy plagues: O grave, I will be thy destruction".
Everlasting Redeemer, please may the spirit of life in Christ Jesus, which has delivered me from the law of sin and death, minister healing, deliverance, and eternal life to me through the Holy Spirit in Jesus' name.

Psalm 91:10 reads:
"There shall no evil befall thee, neither shall any plague come nigh thy dwelling."
Most merciful God, please, those sins in my life that are responsible for Your promise in the Word not to be fulfilled, I repent of them genuinely, and plead for forgiveness. Please let not the arrow of the enemy locate my dwelling place or let evil befall me all the days of my life in Jesus' name.

Isaiah 40:31 reads:

"But they that wait upon the LORD shall renew their strength; they shall mount up with wings as eagles; they shall run, and not be weary; and they shall walk, and not faint."

Father Lord, Jehovah Rapha, I stand on Your word. Please let Your anointing renew my strength, health, spirit, soul, and body, in Jesus' name.

Proverbs 9:11 reads:

"For by me thy days shall be multiplied, and the years of thy life shall be increased."

O Holy God of multiplicity and increase, please multiply my years and increase me in every area of my life in Jesus' name.

Matthew 8:2–3 reads:

"And, behold, there came a leper and worshipped him, saying, Lord, if thou wilt, thou canst make me clean. And Jesus put forth his hand, and touched him, saying I will; be thou clean. And immediately his leprosy was cleansed."

Jehovah Rapha, my great Healer, I believe that if you can point at this my infirmity with Your white finger, it will disappear. Please God, let my faith make me whole in Jesus' name.

2 Corinthians 12:9 reads:

"And he said unto me, My grace is sufficient for thee: for

my strength is made perfect in weakness. Most gladly therefore will I rather glory in my infirmities, that the power of Christ may rest upon me."

My Father and my God, please let these words of Yours accomplish what it is purposed to accomplish in my life. Let Your strength be made perfect in my sickness, in the name of Jesus. As my faith in the unmerited favour and power of God is exercised, let me not be found wanting in Jesus' name.

Galatians 3:13–14 reads:
"Christ hath redeemed us from the curse of the law, being made a curse for us: for it is written, Cursed is everyone that hangeth on a tree: that the blessing of Abraham might come on the Gentiles through Jesus Christ; that we might receive the promise of the Spirit through faith." Every affliction in your life is a curse, but Christ has delivered us from them all through His shed blood. Pray seriously like this:
Spirit of death, infirmity, sickness, disease, poverty, failure, stagnancy, backwardness, etc., you are a curses. Christ has redeemed me from you.
I bind you and cast you away in the mighty name of Jesus Christ. I claim my blessing and healing by faith as they are made available to me through Abraham, my father, by the blood of Jesus and what Christ stands for. I claim restoration in Jesus' name.

Numbers 14:18 reads:

"The LORD is long-suffering, and of great mercy, forgiving iniquity and transgression". For in the book of Romans 9:15 He spoke.

Romans 9:15 reads:

"For he saith to Moses, I will have mercy on whom I will have mercy, and I will have compassion on whom I will have compassion."

Most merciful God, please have mercy on me in this my afflictions; and relieve me of them, so that I can concentrate on my work for You in the name of Jesus. Please do not let Your abundant mercy pass me by in the name of Jesus. Let the blood of Jesus, the power in the name of Jesus, the fire of the Holy Spirit, operate to Your glory in my health in the name of Jesus.

In John 11:25–26

"Jesus said unto her, I am the resurrection, and the life: he that believeth in me, though he were dead, yet shall he live: And whosoever liveth, and believeth in me shall never die".

Most merciful God, please let Your resurrection power minister new life to me, and let my health come alive today in the name of Jesus.

Jesus said in Matthew 18:18b

"And whatsoever ye shall loose on earth shall be loosed in heaven."

I loose myself from all afflictions, sicknesses, and diseases in the name of Jesus.

I also stand on the word of God in Isaiah 53:5 which reads:
"But He was wounded for our transgressions, he was bruised for our iniquities: the chastisement of our peace was upon him; and with his stripes we are healed."
I loose the spirit in these words for operation according to John 6:63 and declare as follows:
In the name of Jesus, satan, Jesus has borne my afflictions, sicknesses, and infirmities on the cross. Therefore, you demons responsible for these ailments, I bind you and cast you away forever to the uninhabitable places in the name of Jesus. I claim my healing in Jesus' name.

Zechariah 4:6 reads:
"Not by might, nor by power, but by my spirit, saith the LORD of hosts."
Holy God of hosts, please let the fire of the Holy Ghost always chase away all my enemies permanently in the name of Jesus. Almighty and Everlasting God, please let the power that commanded Lazarus to come forth; the same power that moulded the sand and carefully pressed it on the eye of the blind man, and his eyes were opened; that power that dried up the 12 year evil flow of the woman with the issue of blood, now minister healing to my health in the name of Jesus.

Psalm 34:19–20
"Many are the afflictions of the righteous: but the Lord

delivereth him from them all.

He keepeth all his bones: not one of them is broken."

Jehovah Rapha, my great Physician, please let my bones be preserved healthy unto Your heavenly kingdom in Jesus' name.

Psalm 91:9–10 reads:

"Because thou hast made the LORD, which is thy refuge, even the Most High, thy habitation; There shall no evil befall thee, neither shall any plague come nigh thy dwelling."

O God, my Refuge and Habitation, please create a fire around me, so that the enemy can neither enter nor dwell inside my body in the name of Jesus.

Jehovah Rapha, please uphold me with Your healing hand of mercy. Do not allow the enemy to plant any sickness in my body in Jesus' name. Please empower me to eat and live right in Jesus' name.

Make the following declarations on your legs:

Psalm 34:20 reads:

"He keepeth all his bones, not one of them is broken."

God gave me these legs for His work. Therefore, no weapon fashioned against my legs shall prosper, in Jesus' name. I pass the decree that these my legs will not glorify Satan but glorify God in Jesus' name.

Moses in his very old age never experienced pain on the legs to our knowledge.

O Holy God, please let the spirit of pain currently attacking the legs of the elderly people be spiritually set ablaze with fire in Jesus' name. Now, challenge that spirit and your legs with the fire of the Holy Ghost for a considerable length of time. Also, challenge it with the blood of Jesus. Let it flow into your bones and marrow. You will discover that most of the pain is spiritual and will begin to disappear, in Jesus' name.

Thank God for answered prayers.

Prayers for the Healing of the Eyes

The eye is a very vital organ in the body and controls multifarious functions. If anything happens to it, the individual is cut off from most of the relevant activities in this world. This is why any sickness in the eye is taken very seriously. These sicknesses can be spiritual or physical. The scripture in Matthew 6:22–23 reads:

"The light of the body is the eye: if therefore thine eye be single, thy whole body shall be full of light. But if thine eye be evil, thy whole body shall be full of darkness."

Since Christ is for me, I will not experience spiritual darkness, and no weapon of physical darkness fashioned against me shall prosper, in the name of Jesus. Remember to do praise-worship and forgiveness prayers before these prayers.

Psalm 27:7–9 reads:

"Hear O LORD, when I cry with my voice: have mercy also upon me and answer me.

When thou saidst, Seek ye my face; my heart said unto

thee, Thy face, LORD, will I seek. Hide not thy face from me; put not thy servant away in anger: thou hast been my help; leave me not, neither forsake me, O God of my salvation."

The mighty Healer, Jehovah Rapha, please if there is any sin in my life that will prevent Your answering this prayer, have mercy and forgive. I repent of them all in Jesus' name.

Anywhere that my eyes have been tied by the kingdom of darkness, O Holy God, please let them be loosed in the name of Jesus.

Deuteronomy 34:7

"And Moses was an hundred and twenty years old when he died: his eye was not dim, nor his natural force abated."

I thank You, most merciful God, for that hand of power that sustained the eyes and strength of Moses over the years. Holy Father, You are the same yesterday, today, and forever. Please release the same anointing for my eyes and my strength, so that I can do your work well on this earth in the name of Jesus.

Ezra 9:8 reads:

"That our GOD may lighten our eyes, and give us a little reviving in our bondage."

Everlasting Redeemer, You are the one who lights my candle and enlightens my darkness. Please release Your healing touch on my eyes, so that their healthy condition will be revived in Jesus' name. I declare that no weapon of cataract or glaucoma fashioned against me shall prosper because my eyes will glorify the Holy God whom I worship. I bind these spirits, and cast them away in Jesus' name. Alternatively, O God, You can perform a creative operation in my eyes in order to put right what is wrong in the name of Jesus.

Isaiah 29:18 reads:
"And in that day shall the deaf hear the words of the book, and the eyes of the blind shall see out of obscurity, and out of darkness."
O God of miracles, signs, and wonders, please let all the demons of the eyes programmed against my eyes be permanently uprooted, in the name of Jesus.

Isaiah 32:3 reads:
"And the eyes of them that see shall not be dim, and the ears of them that hear shall hearken."
Father Lord, I stand on this scripture and declare that no weapon of the dimness of eyes fashioned against me shall prosper in the name of Jesus.

Isaiah 35:5 reads:
"Then the eyes of the blind shall be opened, and the ears of the deaf shall be unstopped."
Eternal Deliverer, You are the Physician, the Medication, and the Power, please let my eyes enjoy the divine health promised it in the name of Jesus. Let any power challenging the power of God in my eyes fail permanently in the name of Jesus.

Isaiah 42:7 reads:

"To open the blind eyes, to bring out the prisoners from the prison, and them that sit in the darkness out of the prison house."

Eternal King of Glory, the great Restorer, please let any part of my eyes that is subject to attack and is malfunctioning be restored to perfect health in the name of Jesus.

Psalm 13:3 reads:

"Consider and hear me O LORD my God: lighten mine eyes, lest I sleep the sleep of death."

O Holy God, my great Physician, please quicken my eyes with your fire, so that the vitality of life will be fully restored there in Jesus' name. Let every spirit of cataract or glaucoma in my eyes be permanently uprooted in Jesus' name.

Psalm 25:15 reads:

"Mine eyes are ever toward the LORD; for he shall pluck my feet out of the net."

Everlasting Father, You are my light and salvation, please restore sound health and vision to my eyes in the name of Jesus.

Psalm 27:4 reads:

"One thing have I desired of the LORD, that will I seek after; that I may dwell in the house of the LORD all the days of my life, to behold the beauty of the LORD, and to enquire in his temple."

Jehovah Rapha, You are the God that heals me, and with You, all things are possible. Please put my eyes right, so that I can behold Your glory and enquire in Your temple in Jesus' name.

Psalm 54:7 reads:
"For he hath delivered me out of all trouble: and mine eye hath seen his desire upon mine enemies."
Merciful God of all goodness, please let my eyes experience Your touch of power, so that my enemies will perceive Your glory in the name of Jesus.

Psalm 91:8 reads:
"Only with thine eyes shalt thou behold and see the reward of the wicked."
Father Lord, by Your great power, please keep my eyes in perfect health, so that I can see the outcome of my attackers in the name of Jesus.

Psalm 121:1–2 reads:
"I will lift up mine eyes unto the hills, from whence cometh my help, my help cometh from the LORD, which made heaven and earth."
O Thou great Physician, the Author of life and health, I lift up my eyes to You, my hope is based on You. Please let my eyes receive Your healing touch in the name of Jesus.

Psalm 123:2 reads:

"Behold, as the eyes of servants look unto the hand of their masters, and as the eyes of a maiden unto the hand of her mistress; so our eyes wait upon the LORD our God, until that he have mercy upon us."

O Lord, my Everlasting Deliverer, my soul yearns for Your power and glory. Please release Your anointing of healing on my eyes in the name of Jesus.

Proverbs 4:25 reads:

"Let thine eyes look right on, and let thine eyelids look straight before thee."

Holy God, I know that You will deliver me from every evil work. Please heal my eyes, so that they can be properly focused on You and looking straight before You in Jesus' name.

Proverbs 23:26 reads:

"My son, give me thine heart, and let thine eyes observe my ways." In Jesus' Name.

Jehovah Rapha, my great Physician, please let my heart and eyes be focused only on you, so that You can always deliver my eyes from the plan of the wicked as I work in Your ways in Jesus' name.

Ezekiel 20:7 reads:

"Then said I unto them, Cast ye away everyman the abominations of his eyes".

Holy Spirit of the living God, please empower me to keep my eyes away from any evil, so that the healing power of

God can flow into them in Jesus' name.

Matthew 9:29–30 reads:
"Then touched he their eyes, saying, According to your faith be it unto you. And their eyes were opened".
Jehovah Rapha, my great Healer, I know that wherever You lay Your hands on, deliverance takes place. Please lay your hands of fire and power on my eyes, so that according to my faith, I may be made whole in Jesus' name.

Make the following confessions and personalize them:
With my eyes, I can read and study the Word, perceive things, win souls for God, and advance the course of evangelism. Therefore, no weapon fashioned against my eyes shall prosper in Jesus' name (Isaiah 54:17).
My eyes will not experience blindness because it is always focused on and working for the Lord in Jesus' name (Psalm 25:15).

Jeremiah 17:14 reads:
"Heal me, O LORD, and I shall be healed: save me, and I shall be saved: for thou art my praise."
Heal my eyes, O Holy God, and deliver me from all the attacks of the enemy in the name of Jesus.

Pray like this:
Psalm 24:7 "Lift up your heads, O ye gates (**of my eyes**); and be ye lifted up ye everlasting doors (**of my eyes**); and the King of glory shall come in. Who is this King of

glory? The LORD strong and mighty, the LORD mighty in battle."

Psalm 27:2 "When the wicked, even mine enemies and my foes, came upon me to eat up my flesh, they stumbled and fell."

Father of all mercies, please let all the enemies that are attacking my eyes stumble and fall in Jesus' name.

Psalm 34:19 "Many are the afflictions of the righteous: but the LORD delivereth him out of them all. He keepeth all his bones, not one of them is broken."

Father God, please deliver my eyes from every evil work, and preserve them unto Your everlasting kingdom in Jesus Name (2 Timothy 4:18).

John 1:5 "And the light shineth in darkness; and the darkness comprehended it not."

O God, please let Your light shine in my eyes, and let not the darkness comprehend it, in Jesus' name.

"I will lift up mine eyes unto the hills, from whence cometh my help. My help cometh from the Lord, which made heaven and earth. He will not suffer thy foot to be moved" (Psalm 121:1–3).

The Holy God that made heaven and earth, please do not let my eyes receive any arrow from the enemy in the name of Jesus.

Isaiah 53:5 reads:

"But he was wounded for our transgressions, he was bruised for our iniquities: the chastisement for our peace

was upon him; and with his stripes we are healed."
I stand on Your word, O Holy God of my salvation, and I claim healing for my eyes, in the name of Jesus. I bind and cast away the spirit of eye trouble in the name of Jesus. Thank God for answered prayers, in Jesus' name.

Chapter 5

PRAYERS AGAINST SELF-DESTRUCTION

Reasons for Depression and Suicide

Depression is very prevalent among the youths of today. Uncontrolled anxiety leads to depression. Extreme depression leads to suicide.

There are many things that can cause depression in the lives of people and these include the following:
- Abuse or violence in the home,
- Family break up
- Frustration over lack of a secure place to live in
- Prolonged unemployment
- Very discouraging student loan scheme
- Exam pressure
- Bullying
- Dangerous Internet programmes
- Racial and hate crimes
- Perilous times
- Polluted and sexualized world

The Church

In the book of Luke 12:25-26, and 31, it is written: "And which of you with taking thought can add to his stature one cubit? If ye then be not able to do that thing which is least, why take ye thought for the rest? … But rather seek ye first the kingdom of God (and its righteousness); and all these things shall be added unto you."

The responsibility to prevent extreme depression which leads to suicide is that of the family, the community, the state, the government, and the church. Although the contributions of these organisations can be of immense impact, it is largely and definitely the church, which is the body of Christ, that can get rid of the very spirit responsible for a serious suicide case through the process of deliverance prayers. The other bodies may have a taming effect.

This spirit of deceit, possesses the mind and thoughts of its victims leading them into acts of suicide or schizophrenia. Suicide suddenly terminates any chance that one has of repenting and preparing for heaven. This act invites the wrath of God.

In the book of Psalm 107:20, the Word of God says, "He sent his word, and healed them, and delivered them from their destructions."

In the book of Hebrews 11:6, it is written that "But without faith it is impossible to please him: for he that cometh to God must believe that he is, and that he is a rewarder of them that diligently seek him." Also, in John 6:63, Jesus said, "The words that I speak unto you, they are spirit, and they are life". From these scriptures, it can be seen that deliverance from this spirit of extreme depression or suicide can come as a result of knowing and obeying the Word of God and reposing faith in the Lord Jesus Who defeated it at the Cross of Calvary.

Having repented and confessed your sins before God, accept Jesus as Lord and Saviour in a Bible believing Church. You will be baptised. Rom.6:3–4. As deliverance prayers are said, believe that God through His Son, Jesus Christ, is able to deliver or heal you.

Maybe you believe that you have nothing more to live for in this world. The love of Jesus that made Him pay the penalty for your sin with His blood is worth your living for. It will also free you from that satanic spirit of suicide. The consequence of committing suicide is death. In Exodus 20:13, the Word of God clearly states: "Thou shall not kill." This includes yourself.

Jesus said, "These things I have spoken to you, that in Me you may have peace. In the world you will have tribulation; but be of good cheer, I have overcome the world" (John 16:33 NKJV).

Claim the victory that Jesus has won for you by faith. Give that life to Christ. He will make it victorious for you. Since God is always willing, able, and waiting to forgive. Belong to the household of God.

In Ezekiel 18:4 (NKJV), God said to Zerubbabel, "Behold, all souls are mine ... the soul that sinneth shall die." Life in hell fire can never be a better option for any suffering on this earth!

The ministry of Christ on earth, which He handed over to the Church with the necessary power through the Holy Spirit, is stated in the book of Luke 4:18–19, and it says: "The Spirit of the Lord is upon me, because He has anointed me to preach the gospel to the poor; He has sent me to heal the broken hearted, to preach deliverance to the captives, and the recovering of sight to the blind, to set at liberty them that are bruised, to preach the acceptable year of the Lord."
You can identify your problem here, which is the need to receive liberty from the oppressive spirit of extreme depression and suicide.

The Consequences of Committing Suicide
Exodus 20:13 reads: "Thou shall not kill." The God whom you will immediately come face to face with if you commit suicide has decreed this. Will He forgive you?
Ezekiel 18:4 reads: "Behold, all souls are mine; as the soul of the father, so also the soul of the son is mine: the soul that sinneth, it shall die." This is the second death. Nobody has the right to sever the soul created from his or her body.

Jesus said in Matthew 10:28 "And fear not them which kill the body, but are not able to kill the soul: but rather fear him which is able to destroy both soul and body in hell." There is nothing worse than spending one's life in a fire that burns and never stops. It is also not advisable to hasten one's stay there whether consciously or unconsciously. The victim of suicide has suddenly terminated the chance of preparing for heaven in order to escape 'hell on earth'.

Prayers Against Depression and Suicide

Mark 11:24 reads: "What thingsoever ye desire, when you pray, believe that you receive them and you shall have them."

In Mark 9:23–24, Jesus said: "If thou canst believe, all things are possible to him that believeth. And straightway the father of the child cried out, and said with tears, Lord, I believe; help thou mine unbelief."

Holy God, the Author and Finisher of my faith, have mercy on me. Please cast away this spirit of extreme depression and suicide from me, and set me free from the bondage of death and hell in the name of Jesus.

In Matthew 15:13, Jesus said: "Every plant, which my heavenly Father hath not planted, shall be rooted up."

Everlasting Deliverer, please let any tree which God has not planted in my life, responsible for the tendency of me to try to terminate my life, be uprooted permanently from me in the name of Jesus.

Hebrews 8:10 reads:

"For this is the covenant that I will make with the house of Israel after those days, saith the Lord; I will put my laws in their mind, and write them in their hearts: and I will be to them a God and they shall be to me a people."

O Holy God, the Strength of my life, let Your new covenant of grace and mercy bring repentance and remission of sin into my mind, so that I can receive divine health and be in control of the thoughts of my mind again in Jesus' name.

Most blessed spirit of the living God, please let your fire lighten and electrify Your laws in my mind, so that they can burn off all the thoughts trying to challenge the word of God in there in the name of Jesus.

Proverbs 21:1 reads:

"The King's heart is in the hand of the LORD; as the rivers of water he turneth it whithersoever he will."

O Holy God of miracles, signs, and wonders, please take control of my thoughts, and turn it to be focused on the things of the Spirit in Jesus' name.

Psalm 94:11–12

"The Lord knows the thoughts of man, that they are vanity. Blessed is the man whom you chastenest, O Lord, and teachest out of thy law."

O Holy God, the Creator of knowledge, please let any enemy; human or spiritual, foundational or cultural, forcing my thoughts to go against Your will, fail permanently in the name of Jesus.

Psalm 118:17 reads:

"I shall not die, but live, and declare the works of the Lord in the land of the living."

Jehovah Nisi, the mighty Warrior, please let any spirit of death and hell trying to terminate my destiny receive Your resistance and fail permanently in Jesus' name.

Psalm 51:14 reads:

"Deliver me from bloodguiltiness, O God, thou God of my salvation."

Everlasting God, to whom belongs the power to extend days and multiply years, please, I truly repent of the sin of contemplating to take my life. Forgive me and empower me through the Holy Spirit to attain eternal life in the name of Jesus.

Hebrews 9:14 reads:

"How much more shall the blood of Christ who through the eternal Spirit offered himself without spot to God, purge your conscience from dead works to serve the living God?"

The Holy God, the Foundation of all truth, please let the spiritual sacrifice of the innocent blood of Jesus Christ cleanse my thoughts and conscience from dead thoughts and works in the name of Jesus.

Revelation 12:11 reads:

"And they overcame him by the blood of the Lamb, and by the word of their testimony; and they loved not their lives unto death."

I plead the blood of Jesus on my mind and in my thoughts in the name of Jesus (continue until you feel a release).

O God, please let the power in the blood of Jesus that availed for me at the cross of Calvary flush out every thought of death and hell from my mind, in the name of Jesus.

Matthew 15:19 reads:
"For out of the heart proceed evil thoughts".
O Holy God of battle, please let any power that is injecting fear and panic into my thoughts fail and be ejected from my life in the name of Jesus.

Psalm 94:11–12 reads:
"The LORD knoweth the thoughts of man, that they are vanity. Blessed is the man whom thou chastenest, O LORD, and teachest him out of thy law; That thou mayest give him rest from the days of adversity, until the pit be digged for the wicked."
O Jehovah, God, please let the sanctifying power of the Holy Spirit cleanse and sanctify my heart unto eternal, and empower me to accept criticisms, corrections and change, in Jesus' name.

Psalm 16:4–5 reads:
"Their drink offerings of blood will I not offer, nor take up their names into my lips. The LORD is the portion of mine inheritance and my cup".
You, satanic spirit of suicide, Jesus has already shed his blood for me. Therefore, I owe you nothing. According

to the Word of God in Romans 8:2, "For the law of the Spirit of life in Christ Jesus hath made me free from the law of sin and death."

Psalm 18:44–45 reads:
"As soon as they hear of me, they obey me: the strangers shall submit themselves unto me. The strangers shall fade away, and be afraid out of their close places."
I plead the blood of Jesus on my spirit, soul, and body in the name of Jesus.
O Holy God, our High Tower and Deliverer, please let the satanic spirit of extreme depression be challenged and driven away by the power in the blood of Jesus and the fire of the Holy Spirit in the name of Jesus.

Psalm 107:20 reads:
"He sent his word, and healed them and delivered them from their destructions."
Jehovah Rapha, the God that heals us, please let Your word which is living and powerful, and is like a two-edged sword of fire that pierces even to the dividing of soul and spirit, penetrate into my mind and uproot the satanic spirit of extreme depression that is tending towards suicide in the name of Jesus.

3 John 1:2 reads:
"Beloved, I wish above all things that thou mayest prosper and be in health, even as thy soul prospereth."
O Holy God in whom alone we trust, please as I grow in the wisdom and knowledge of Your word, let this be

commensurate with improvement in my health in the name of Jesus.

 Psalm 11:3 reads:

"If the foundation be destroyed, what will the righteous do?"

Everlasting Father of light, our Salvation, please let any evil transactions of foundational enemies in my dreams that is largely responsible for my mental health be cancelled permanently by the power in the blood of Jesus, in Jesus' name.

Thank You, Holy God, for answered prayers in Jesus' name.

Chapter 6

PROSPERITY

Remember to do praise/worship and forgiveness prayers (as much as you can), before doing these prayers.

Prosperity is one of the plans of redemption for your life. Why should you die poor when God has made available his abundant blessings for your life? The Almighty God Himself who created the entire universe and created Satan, who steals from you the good things He sends, has spoken through John His close disciple in 3 John 1:2 saying, "Beloved, I wish above all things that thou mayest prosper and be in health, even as thy soul prospereth."

God wishes above everything in this world that His children should possess and enjoy immense wealth and good health as a result of the prosperity of their souls. The prosperity of the soul is also closely tied to salvation and holiness. He does not want us to labour in vain. He wants us to enjoy what our father Abraham enjoyed. He never likes to see His children begging and borrowing for this is as a result of sin. If you excel in holiness, you will attract a lot of wealth by the grace of God. What He strongly disapproves of is that your mind will be preoccupied with that wealth. This leads to idolatry. We are told in the scriptures that a man cannot serve two masters.

The scripture tells us in Psalm 24:1 that "The earth is the LORD'S, and the fullness thereof; the world, and they that dwell therein." This means that we can command the devil and his spiritual and human agents to get away from all that belongs to us, which came from our Heavenly Father, the Owner of this whole world, in the name of Jesus. Repeat this prayer of declaration several times until you achieve spiritual peace in it.

Lift up your heads, O ye gates of my progress, and be ye lifted up, ye ancient gates of my health, and the Holy King of provision shall come in. Who is this King of provision and abundance, the Lord, strong and mighty, the Lord, mighty in battle.

Mark 11:24 states:
"What things so ever ye desire, when ye pray, believe that ye receive them, and ye shall have them."
Always ask in faith, holiness, and truth. O God, my Financial Healer, please let all the financial victories which Your right hand has achieved for me spiritually, manifest now physically to Your glory in the mighty name of Jesus.

1 Corinthians 3:21 and 23 reads:

"Therefore let no man glory in men. For all things are yours; and ye are Christ's; and Christ is God's."

If all things are ours and we are Christ's, we should not be poor. The word of God in Joel 2:25 has given us the assurance that the goodness which Satan stole from us can be recovered.

Most merciful God, and the Author of restoration, please let everything that the enemy has stolen from me, which you have authorized to be restored to me, be recovered now in the name of Jesus.

The Word of God in John 6:63 reads:

"The words that I speak unto you, they are Spirit, and they are life."

Matthew 18:18b reads:

"Verily I say unto you, Whatsoever ye shall bind on earth shall be bound in heaven: and whatsoever ye shall loose on earth shall be loosed in heaven."

I stand on these words and pray like this: O Thou covenant-keeping God, whose words are 'Yes' and 'Amen', I bind all satanic spirits and their powers who are trying to terminate Your progress and prosperity in my life in the name of Jesus. I cast them away in Jesus' name. I loose the spirits attached to these words to make sure that they do not come back again in the mighty name of Jesus. I plead the blood of Jesus on these prayers in the name of Jesus.

Matthew 15:13 reads:

"But he answered and said, Every plant, which my heavenly Father hath not planted, shall be rooted up."

By Thy everlasting power, O God, please dig deep into the innermost part of my foundation, and uproot all the evil roots of poverty which the enemy had planted there in the mighty name of Jesus.

John 8:36: reads: "If the Son therefore shall make you free, ye shall be free indeed."

(True freedom is righteousness). Jehovah Jireh, my great Deliverer and Provider, please release Your earthquake of deliverance to deliver me and my family from a foundational bondage of financial poverty in the name of Jesus.

The Word of God says in 2 Corinthians 6:17:

"Wherefore come out from among them, and be ye separate, saith the LORD, and touch not the unclean thing, and I will receive you."

Thou Fountain of truth and righteousness, please let anything in my possession that is unclean and withholding Your blessings from flowing into my life be exposed and removed permanently in the name of Jesus.

Ezekiel 36:36 reads:

"Then the heathen that are left round about you shall know that I the LORD build the ruined places, and plant that that was desolate: I the LORD have spoken it, and I will do it."

Most powerful God and the Author of restoration, please restore my lost possessions and rebuild my ruined places in the name of Jesus.

Matthew 17:20 reads:
"And Jesus said unto them, Because of your unbelief: for verily I say unto you, If ye have faith as a grain of mustard seed, ye shall say unto this mountain, Remove hence to yonder place; and it shall remove; and nothing shall be impossible unto you."
You, satanic mountain of financial difficulty in my life, I stand on the Word of God in Matthew 17:20, and command you in faith to depart immediately from my life in the name of Jesus. You are not the will of God for my life in Jesus' name.

Psalm 1:3 reads:
"And he shall be like a tree planted by the rivers of water, that bringeth forth his fruit in his season; his leaf also shall not wither; and whatsoever he doeth shall prosper."
Thou Holy God, my great Provider, please let me be planted by the rivers of water where I can be well nourished in order to multiply my seeds at the appropriate time. Let my banners be full, affording all manner of stores in Jesus' name.

Luke 6:38 reads:
"Give, and it shall be given unto you; good measure, pressed down, and shaken together, and running over, shall men give into your bosom. For with the same

measure that ye mete withal it shall be measured to you again."

Everlasting Father, please impart in me a willing spirit of generosity, so that I can always reap benefits from Your kingdom as I give in the name of Jesus.

Galatians 3:13–14 reads:

"Christ hath redeemed us from the curse of the law, being made a curse for us: for it is written, Cursed is every one that hangeth on a tree: that the blessing of Abraham might come on the Gentiles through Jesus Christ; that we might receive the promise of the spirit through faith."

Eternal Redeemer and Provider, thank You for salvation. Please may the promise of justification in Abraham, our father by faith, and the Spirit through Christ ever remain with me in Jesus' name. May I also appropriate the wealth of the Gentiles in Jesus' name.

Joel 2:25–26 reads:

"And I will restore to you the years that the locust hath eaten, the cankerworm, and the caterpillar, and the palmerworm, my great army, which I sent among you. And ye shall eat in plenty, and be satisfied, and praise the name of the LORD your God."

My Holy Father and my God, please let my enemies see me possess from them all my stolen blessings which I should repossess, but do not let them steal, kill, or destroy them anymore in the name of Jesus.

Holy God, please direct me through Your Spirit on how to plant in due time and at the right place, so that when the time for the harvest comes, I may reap and not loose in the name of Jesus. Holy God, let me reap and not loose in Jesus' name.

Isaiah 65:22 reads:
They shall not build, and another inhabit; they shall not plant, and another eat: for as the days of a tree are the days of my people, and mine elect shall long enjoy the works of their hands."
Jehovah Jireh, please let any enemy withholding my blessings be uprooted from my blessings in Jesus' name. Let my blessings glorify You, O God, in Jesus' name. Make me to be like a tree planted by the rivers of water that brings forth its fruit in its season, let me live to enjoy the fruits of my hands, in Jesus' name.

Isaiah 43:18–19 reads:
"Remember ye not the former things, neither consider the things of old.
"Behold, I will do a new thing; now it shall spring forth; shall ye not know it? I will even make a way in the wilderness, and rivers in the desert."
Holy God of power and might, please make a new way for me in my finances where there is no way. Please restore Your glory in my finances in Jesus' name.

Jeremiah 30:17 reads:
"For I will restore health unto thee, and I will heal thee of thy wounds, saith the LORD".
O God of life and health, please heal my finances and

health, and let my progress come alive again in the name of Jesus.

Let no weapon fashioned against my blessings and health prosper in Jesus' name. I cover all my blessings and health with the blood of Jesus in Jesus' name.

Deuteronomy 8:18 reads:

"But thou shalt remember the LORD thy God: for it is he that giveth thee power to get wealth, that he may establish his covenant which he swore unto thy fathers, as it is this day."

Jehovah Jireh, my everlasting Provider, please lead me into areas of abundant blessings that I am not aware of in the name of Jesus. Please teach me how to make wealth through the work of my hands, O Lord, and let the covenant which You established with Abraham, my father, be fulfilled in my life in Jesus' name.

Isaiah 65:22 reads: (Personalize this)

"They shall not build, and another inhabit; they shall not plant, and another eat: for as the days of a tree are the days of my people, and mine elect shall long enjoy the work of their hands."

My Holy Father and my God, please do not allow me to waste my labour in order to feed my enemies (spiritual) in Jesus' name. Let all spiritual and physical devourers in my life be chased away permanently by Your fire, in Jesus' name. Repeat several times. I refuse to labour for Satan in Jesus' name. O God, please let anything that will try to deceive or compel me to labour for Satan even in ignorance or in my dreams be permanently uprooted from my life, in the name of Jesus.

Matthew 18:18 reads:
"Verily, verily I say unto you, whatsoever ye shall bind on earth shall be bound in heaven: and whatsoever ye shall loose on earth shall be loosed in heaven."
Father God, I bind and paralyse the spirit of poverty, sin, failure, disappointment, and demonic delay to my progress, and cast them away in Jesus' name.

Psalm 37:4 reads:
"Delight thyself also in the LORD; and he shall give thee the desires of thine heart."
My desire is to do Your will, O Lord. Please grant me the desires of my heart and let them glorify You in my handiwork and life in Jesus' name.

2 Corinthians 8:9 reads:
"For ye know the grace of our LORD Jesus Christ, that, though he was rich, yet for your sakes he became poor, that ye through his poverty might be rich."
Holy Lord Jesus and my Redeemer, You gave up Your wealth in heaven in order to redeem our souls from death. You suffered pain, shame, and poverty for our sakes. As I labour and suffer on this earth, please uphold me, so that I will be able to join you in Heaven in the name of Jesus.

2 Corinthians 9:8 reads:
"And God is able to make all grace abound towards you: that ye, always having all sufficiency in all things, may abound to every good work".
Everlasting Father, please make Your grace sufficient for me, so that I can discharge my responsibilities well as a child of God and anywhere it is needed in the name of Jesus.

Philippians 4:19 reads:
"But my God shall supply all your needs according to His riches in glory by Christ Jesus."
Jehovah Jireh, my only Provider, please let Your promises in the scripture in Philippians 4:19 be fulfilled in my life in Jesus' name.

Psalm 37:18–19 reads:
"The LORD knoweth the days of the upright: and their inheritance shall be forever.
They shall not be ashamed in the evil time: and in the days of famine they shall be satisfied."
O God, please let any sin in my life that will make me ill-qualified for Your blessings be permanently purged from me in the name of Jesus. Let me not labour only to have Satan steal my blessings in Jesus' name.

Proverbs 10:22 reads.
"The blessing of the LORD it maketh rich, and he addeth no sorrow with it."
O God, I also stand on Your Word in Psalm 16:4 which

says that "Their sorrows shall be multiplied that hasten after another god". Please let any sorrow that Satan may try to add to my blessings be made to return back permanently to where it came from in the name of Jesus. I worship You the Lord, my God. You only do I serve. I have no other God beside You; for from You all good things are sent (Jm.1:17).

Psalm 35:27 reads:
"Let them shout for joy, and be glad, that favour my righteous cause: yea, let them say continually, Let the LORD be magnified, which hath pleasure in the prosperity of his servant."
O Holy God, let those who favour my righteous cause have cause to rejoice with me over what You will do in my life in Jesus' name.

Psalm 112:1 reads:
"Praise ye the LORD. Blessed is the man that feareth the LORD, that delighteth greatly in his commandments. His seed shall be mighty upon the earth: the generation of the upright shall be blessed."
I delight in Your commandments, O God, please let Your abundant blessings be upon my life and my generation in Jesus' name.

Psalm 23:5 reads:
"Thou preparest a table before me in the presence of mine enemies: thou anointest my head with oil; my cup runneth over."

O God, please let my enemies live to see how the blessings that You will bestow on my life will glorify You in Jesus' name.

Luke 6:38 reads:
"Give, and it shall be given unto you … For with the same measure that ye mete withal it shall be measured to you again."
Holy God, my Provider, as I give rightly and often, please do not allow the devil, for one reason or the other, to hinder or limit my receiving appropriately in Jesus' name.
O most merciful God, please let the devil's plan for a serious limitation in my blessings fail permanently in Jesus' name.

Psalm 34:8–9 reads:
"O taste and see that the LORD is good: blessed is the man that trusteth in Him. O fear the LORD, ye his saints: for there is no want to them that fear him."
I live in complete fear of You, most merciful God, please do not let me, as Your child, be in want in Jesus' name.

Galatians 3:13–14
"Christ hath redeemed us from the curse of the law, being made a curse for us: for it is written, Cursed is everyone that hangeth on a tree: that the blessing of Abraham might come on the Gentiles through Jesus Christ; that we might receive the promise of the spirit through faith."
In order to receive the promise of abundant blessings

promised Abraham, our father, because of Jesus Christ, we have to operate always on faith and holiness.

Father God, Jehovah, please give me the grace to operate in holiness and faith without wavering, so that Abraham's blessings will be mine in Jesus' name.

Psalm 5:12 reads:

"For thou, LORD, wilt bless the righteous; with favour wilt thou compass him as with a shield."

O Jehovah Jireh the great Provider, please help me to live righteously so that I can receive blessings and favour from You, in the presence of my enemies in the name of Jesus.

Revelation 12:11 reads:

"And they overcame him by the blood of the Lamb, and by the word of their testimony; and they loved not their lives unto the death."

I plead the blood of Jesus on all my prayers and blessings, in the name of Jesus. By the power in the blood of Jesus, I claim all my blessings as a seed of Abraham based on God's promises to him in Jesus' name, and I confess that no weapon fashioned against me or my blessings shall prosper in the name of Jesus.

Confess this prayer:

Jehovah Jireh is my Financial Power, Progress, and Strength. He is my Financial Executor, Banker and Supplier. I shall take no further step away from Him in the name of Jesus. I shall obey all His laws of prosperity and will live in abundance for the rest of my life. The enemy cannot hinder me anymore in the name of Jesus.

Exodus 23:25 reads:
"And ye shall serve the LORD your God, and He shall bless thy bread, and thy water; and I will take sickness away from the midst of thee."
Father God, as I serve You, please attend to my needs and bless my handiwork, in Jesus' name. Please protect my blessings from financial devourers in Jesus' name.

John 15:16 reads:
"Ye have not chosen me, but I have chosen you, and ordained you, that ye should go and bring forth fruit, and that your fruit should remain: that whatsoever ye shall ask of the Father in my name, he may give it you."
Father God, please let any spirit working against my fruitfulness in You receive Your direct opposition and punishment in Jesus' name.
O Holy God, please quicken my spirit man, so that I can bear fruits easily for You in the name of Jesus.

Psalm 18:33 reads:
"He maketh my feet like hinds' feet, and setteth me upon my high places."
Jehovah Jireh, my great Provider, please let any enemy whether spiritual or physical, that is working hard to pull me down or to limit Your blessings of prosperity in my life be frustrated, disappointed, and defeated permanently in the name of Jesus.

2 Corinthians 8:9 reads:

"For ye know the grace of our Lord Jesus Christ, that, though he was rich, yet for your sakes he became poor, that ye through His poverty might be rich."

Eternal King of Glory, please let the exchange You made at the Cross for my prosperity not be in vain in my life and that of my family in the name of Jesus. Let any enemy of my progress, who has made it his preoccupation to reverse any blessing that comes to me, receive permanent resistance from the blood of Jesus, in Jesus' name.

2 Corinthians 9:8 reads:

"And God is able to make all grace abound toward you; that ye, always having all sufficiency in all things, may abound to every good work".

O Holy God, my Provider, please let Your blessing in my life always make me a channel of blessing to others in the name of Jesus.

Job 5:22 reads:

"At destruction and famine thou shalt laugh: neither shalt thou be afraid of the beasts of the earth."

O Thou Holy God of my sufficiency, at this time of wars, depression, and destructive weather conditions, please do not allow my family and I to be in want in the name of Jesus. At this time of end time manifestations, please do not allow us to be deprived or polluted in the name of Jesus.

Psalm 84:11 reads:

"For the LORD God is a sun and shield: the Lord will give grace and glory: no good thing will he withhold from them that walk uprightly."

O God of mercy and truth, as we serve You, please do not withhold the manifestation of Your blessings from us, in the name of Jesus.

John 10:10

"The thief cometh not, but for to steal, and to kill, and to destroy: I am come that they might have life, and that they might have it more abundantly."

O God, the Eternal Source of our lives, please do not allow Satan to steal, kill, or destroy again in our lives in the name of Jesus.

Joshua 1:7 reads:

"Only be thou strong and very courageous, that thou mayest observe to do according to all the law, which Moses my servant commanded thee: turn not from it to the right hand or to the left, that thou mayest prosper whithersoever thou goest."

O God, the Eternal Strength of my life, please enable me to ignore the distractions of this life (sickness, fear, lack of money, lust, worldly standards, satanic deceit, etc.), so that they do not rob me of my prosperity and life in the name of Jesus.

Isaiah 60:17 reads:

"For brass I will bring gold, and for iron I will bring silver and for wood brass, and for stones iron".

Eternal Redeemer, please let my restoration spring up as light and glorify You, my Provider, in the mighty name of Jesus.

Isaiah 60:20 reads:

"Thy sun shall no more go down; neither shall thy moon withdraw itself: for the LORD shall be thine everlasting Light, and the days of thy mourning shall be ended."

Everlasting Father, whose promises are 'Yea' and 'Amen' to Your glory, please let Your promises in Isaiah 60:20 be fulfilled in my life in the name of Jesus.

Psalm 27:1 reads:

"The LORD is my light and my salvation; whom shall I fear? The LORD is the strength of my life, of whom shall I be afraid?"

O Holy God, my Light and my Strength, please give me the grace to operate on a permanent level of holiness and prosperity, so that I will not experience again the days of darkness and mourning in Jesus' name.

Isaiah 60:22 reads:

"A little one shall become a thousand, and a small one a strong nation: I the LORD will hasten it in his time."

By Your everlasting mercies, O God, please let the growth and multiplicity that will glorify You be always my portion in the name of Jesus.

1 Timothy 6:17–18:

"Charge them that are rich in this world, that they be not highminded … That they do good, that they be rich in good works, ready to distribute, willing to communicate."

Thou great Provider, my Father and my God, please let not the spirit of selfishness and pride hinder the ministry of giving in my life in the name of Jesus.

Proverbs 3:9–10 reads:

"Honour the LORD with thy substance, and with the firstfruits of all thine increase. So shall thy barns be filled with plenty, and thy presses shall burst out with new wine."

O Holy God that keeps covenant with them that love Him, please as I honour You with my substance and first fruits, replenish my store house with plenty in the name of Jesus. With the blood of Jesus, I reject and cancel any limitation imposed by the enemy in the name of Jesus.

Exodus 14:21 reads:

"And Moses stretched out his hand over the sea; and the LORD caused the sea to go back by a strong east wind all that night, and made the sea dry land and the waters were divided."

O God of power and might, for my breakthrough, please command satanic obstructions to give way like the Red Sea in the name of Jesus.

Isaiah 62:8 reads:

"The LORD hath sworn by his right hand, and by the arm of his strength, Surely I will no more give thy corn to be meat for thine enemies; and the sons of the stranger shall not drink thy wine; for which thou last laboured".

O most merciful and righteous Judge, please do not let me build and another inhabit; let me not plant and another eat, and let me not labour in vain in this world in Jesus' name.

Isaiah 62:9 reads: "But they that have gathered it shall eat it, and praise the LORD; and they that have brought it together shall drink it in the courts of my holiness."

Everlasting Father of Glory, please let me have cause to praise, worship, and glorify You with the labour of my hands in Jesus' name.

Obadiah 1:17 reads:

"But upon mount Zion shall be deliverance, and there shall be holiness; and the house of Jacob shall possess their possessions."

Eternal God, my Provider, as I have received salvation, please give me the grace to live a holy life, so that I can repossess my possessions in Jesus' name.

Isaiah 62:11 reads:

"Behold, the LORD hath proclaimed unto the end of the world, Say ye to the daughter of Zion, Behold, thy salvation cometh; behold, his reward is with him, and his work before him."

Everlasting Father, my light and my salvation, please do not allow me to run this race in vain, in Jesus' name. Let my reward be made manifest to me in Jesus' name.

Proverbs 11:27 reads:
"He that diligently seeketh good procureth favour: but he that seeketh mischief, it shall come unto him."
My everlasting Father, please give me the grace to follow the path of goodness and favour, all the days of my life in Jesus' name.

Proverbs 11:25 reads:
"The liberal soul shall be made fat: and he that watereth shall be watered also himself."
Father Lord, You are the greatest Giver, please empower me to follow Your example and be very willing to release my gifts and goodness not only for Your service but to the needy in Jesus' name.

Isaiah 41:18, 20 reads:
"I will open rivers in high places, and fountains in the midst of the valleys: I will make the wilderness a pool of water, and the dry land springs of water.
"That they may see, and know, and consider, and understand together, that the hand of the LORD hath done this, and the Holy One of Israel hath created it."
Jehovah Jireh, my great Provider, please make the financially impossible possible for me to Your glory, in Jesus' name. Please for Your service, open windows of opportunities for me in Jesus' name.

Psalm 113:5, 7–8 reads:

"Who is like unto the LORD our God, who dwelleth on high.

"He raiseth up the poor out of the dust, and lifteth the needy out of the dunghill; that he may set him with princes, even with the princes of his people."

O Holy God, my Advancer, please propel me upwards by Your great power in the name of Jesus; and as You lift me up, empower me also to grow in holiness and humility in Jesus' name.

Psalm 126:5–6 reads:

"They that sow in tears shall reap in joy. He that goeth forth and weepeth, bearing precious seed, shall doubtless come again with rejoicing, bringing his sheaves with him."

O God of power, our Provider and Rewarder, please let the labour of my hands receive adequate reward in the name of Jesus.

Proverbs 13:22 reads:

"A good man leaveth an inheritance to his children's children; and the wealth of the sinner is laid up for the just."

O Holy God of all comfort, please teach me how to build in righteousness. Let not my handiwork be a waste in this world, in Jesus' name. Make me to leave an inheritance for my children's children in Jesus' name.

Psalm 112:2–3 reads:

"His seed shall be mighty upon the earth: the generation of the upright shall be blessed.

Wealth and riches shall be in his house and his righteousness endureth for ever."

O righteous God, please let Your abundant blessing be bestowed on my house and be permanent in Jesus' name. Give me the grace to dwell always in Your righteousness in Jesus' name.

John 10:10 reads:

"The thief cometh not, but for to steal, and to kill, and to destroy: I am come that they might have life, and that they might have it more abundantly."

Merciful God of all provision and comfort, please let all my possessions be preserved from the enemies who kill, destroy, and devour in the name of Jesus.

Psalm 138:8 reads:

"The LORD will perfect that which concerneth me: thy mercy, O LORD, endureth forever; forsake not the works of thine own hands."

O Holy God who has started a good thing in my life, please perfect it to Your glory in the name of Jesus.

Proverbs 28:20 reads:

"A faithful man shall abound with blessings: but he that maketh haste to be rich shall not be innocent."

Holy God of abundant blessings, please guide me away from the path that leads to hastily and ill-gotten wealth.

Enable me to wait faithfully and patiently for You to prove Yourself in my life in Jesus' name.

Psalm 34:10 reads:
"The young lions do lack, and suffer hunger: but they that seek the LORD shall not want any good thing."
Thou great Provider, please as I run this race looking towards You alone, please do not let me be in need of any relevant blessings in the name of Jesus.

Psalm 23:5 reads:
"Thou preparest a table before me in the presence of mine enemies: thou anointest my head with oil; my cup runneth over."
My Holy Father and my God, the One who is able to do exceeding abundantly above all that we ask or think, please release Your abundant blessing in my life in Jesus' name.

Psalm 113:7–8 reads:
"He raiseth up the poor out of the dust, and lifteth the needy out of the dunghill;
That he may set him with princes, even with the princes of his people."
O Holy God that uplifts those who trust, believe, and serve Him, even to the highest heights of blessings that are imaginable, please do not pass me by in Your goodness and mercy in Jesus' name.

Deuteronomy 8:7–9 reads:

"For the LORD thy God bringeth thee into a good land, … a land of wheat, and barley, and vines, and fig trees, and pomegranates; a land of oil olive and honey; a land wherein thou shalt eat bread without scarceness, thou shalt not lack anything in it".

Holy Father, it is clear that with holiness and righteousness, I shall inherit Your blessings. O Great Provider, Jehovah Jireh, please lead me to a state of goodness and abundance where I can use my resources to provide services for You and Your church and be able to lend to many nations in the name of Jesus.

Deuteronomy 8:12–14a reads:

"Lest when thou hast eaten and art full, and hast built goodly houses, and dwell therein; and when thy herds and thy flocks multiply, and thy silver and thy gold is multiplied, and all that thou hast is multiplied; then thine heart be lifted up, and thou forget the LORD thy God".

O Holy God that keepeth covenant with them that love Him, please do not allow the spirit of pride of success and self-exaltation to consume me and turn my heart away from my obligations and services for You in the name of Jesus.

Psalm 35:27b reads:

"Let the LORD be magnified, which hath pleasure in the prosperity of his servant."

O Holy God who delights in the prosperity of His

servants, please let Your good thoughts towards me attract prosperity into my life in the name of Jesus.

Let my prosperity glorify You in Jesus' name.

Job 36:11 reads:

"If they obey and serve him, they shall spend their days in prosperity, and their years in pleasures."

Thou great and mighty God, who performs great miracles in the lives of Your children, please let any satanic device that will bring disobedience into my life be diverted away from me permanently in the name of Jesus.

Isaiah 43:19 reads:

"Behold, I will do a new thing; now it shall spring forth; shall ye not know it? I will even make a way in the wilderness, and rivers in the desert."

My God, my Shepherd, and my Provider, He who makes a way where there is no way, please do a new thing in my finances that will glorify You, and make my enemies develop a genuine fear of You in the name of Jesus.

End this section with the following prayers:

At this end time, O Lord, a time of hunting for souls, please let not the worldly standard lure me away from You, my Creator.

O Holy God, please do not let the tearful intercessions of Jesus and the blood of preservation be in vain on my life in Jesus' name.

Please give me the determination to make your standard for heaven, and let any enemy, whether human or spiritual, trying to frustrate my efforts fail permanently in the name of Jesus.

Thank You, God, for answered prayers, in Jesus' name.

Chapter 7

EVIL FOUNDATION

Your foundation is your root. It can be the power of ancestral spirits in operation in your life. If the foundation is Christian by origin, there will be minimal problem; but if it is occult, marine, etc., the battle becomes that of life and death. This will determine the seriousness of the prayers you are supposed to be praying. You will need to cry out to God continually to deliver you from foundational attacks.

Psalm 91:5–6 reads:
"Thou shalt not be afraid for the terror by night; nor for the arrow that flieth by day; nor for the pestilence that walketh in the darkness; nor for the destruction that wasteth at noonday."
These verses confirm the fact that a spiritual battle is in operation, and it is only God that can deliver one from it. Pray these prayers standing or kneeling down. Firstly, do as much of the Praise, Worship, and Forgiveness prayers.

Psalm 11:3 reads:

"If the foundations be destroyed, what can the righteous do?" They will continue fervently in prayers.

O holy and mighty God, please empower me to pray without ceasing until the evil foundations of my father, mother, and husband's houses are defeated and changed to that of the Lord Jesus Christ in Jesus' name.

1 Corinthians 3:11 reads:

"For other foundation can no man lay than that is laid, which is Jesus Christ."

O most holy and powerful God, please let any evil foundation in my life laid by Satan, be continually challenged by the blood of Jesus and the fire of the Holy Ghost, in the name of Jesus.

The great Deliverer of our souls, please let the blood of Jesus and the fire of the Holy Ghost eat into the evil foundation of our families and change it permanently in the name of Jesus.

Deuteronomy 33:27 reads:

"The eternal God is thy refuge, and underneath are the everlasting arms: and he shall thrust out the enemy from before thee; and shall say, Destroy them."

O Holy God of war, please by Your power, use me as a vessel to attack and defeat my foundational enemies both in life and in the dream in the name of Jesus.

Isaiah 49:25–26 reads:

"But thus saith the LORD, Even the captives of the mighty

shall be taken away and the prey of the terrible shall be delivered: for I will contend with him that contendeth with thee, and I will save thy children. And I will feed them that oppress thee with their own flesh; and they shall be drunken with their own blood as with sweet wine: and all flesh shall know that I the LORD am thy Saviour and thy Redeemer, the Mighty One of Jacob."

Jehovah Nisi, the mighty God in battle, please let all those held captive by the evil foundation of my family's house be loosed permanently in the name of Jesus; for it is written in John 5:36 that "If the Son therefore shall make you free, ye shall be free indeed."

Psalm 5:4–6 reads;

"For thou art not a God that hath pleasure in wickedness: neither shall evil dwell with thee. The foolish shall not stand in thy sight: thou hatest all workers of iniquity. Thou shalt destroy them that speak leasing: the LORD will abhor the bloody and deceitful man."

Eternal God of all righteousness, Jehovah God, let all the evil wickedness of spiritual foundational enemies and their numerous agents released every day against me be laid out before You, and receive Your urgent attention in Jesus' name. Please In the name of our Lord Jesus Christ, deal with them that have no repentance according to their evil ways. Let all the evil actors and actresses in this evil foundation, which You did not plant, be uprooted permanently in the name of Jesus.

It is written in 2 Corinthians 5:17 that:

"If any man be in Christ, he is a new creature: old things are passed away; behold all things are become new."

Eternal Redeemer, please let the power in the blood of Jesus break permanently any covenant entered between the evil foundational spiritual enemies and my ancestors. Let them become powerless in our lives, in the mighty name of Jesus. I use the blood of Jesus to break any satanic covenant in my life in the name of Jesus.

Psalm 129:4 reads:

"The LORD is righteous: he hath cut asunder the cords of the wicked."

O Holy God of power and might, please let the evil stronghold mounted in the hearts of the evil foundation of the enemy be pulled down by Your word and the fire of the Holy Ghost in Jesus' name.

Esther 7:6–7 reads:

"And Esther said, 'The adversary and enemy is this wicked Haman.' Then Haman was afraid before the king and the queen. And the King arising from the banquet of wine in his wrath went into the palace garden: and Haman stood up to make request for his life to Esther the queen; for he saw that there was evil determined against him by the king."

O Holy God of war and peace, You make and unmake, let that strongman in my family, who has vowed that I and my family must give way, receive the spirit of repentance, in the name of Jesus. If he repents, let him be forgiven; but if he refuses, let Your righteous judgment come upon him now in the name of Jesus.

O God, please withhold, defeat, and put him away from our lives in the name of Jesus.

Exodus 9:1 reads:

"Then the LORD said unto Moses, Go in unto Pharaoh, and tell him, thus saith the LORD God of the Hebrews, let my people go, that they may serve me."

O Holy God, our strong Tower, our Refuge, and our Fortress, please, let the ancestral spirits that are enraged against us and are still attacking us day and night because of our salvation receive a greater measure of Your punishment and fail permanently in Jesus' name.

2 King 2:14b reads:

"Where is the LORD GOD of Elijah? And when he also had smitten the waters, they parted hither and thither and Elisha went over."

I hold the sword of the Spirit in my right hand, and I smite all my problems; I command them to depart in Jesus' name (Pray three times). Then ask; Where, O where is the Lord God of Abraham, Isaac, and Jacob? Please fight for me. Please command all foundational bondages in my life to break in Jesus' name.

Let any access to my dreams be shut to the spirits of idolatry in my foundation in Jesus' name.

Zechariah 4:7 reads:

"Who art thou, O mountain? Before Zerubbabel, thou

shalt become a plain."

Who are you, you spirit of idolatry? Before the only Holy God whom I serve, you shall crumble to the ground in the name of Jesus.

Drum this seven times: O God, please let the spirit of foundational bondage crumble to the ground, now, in Jesus' name. Drum this last sentence seven times: O Holy God, please let any spirit of unconscious idolatry in my foundation be exposed, defeated, and permanently uprooted in the name of Jesus.

Exodus 20:3 reads:

"Thou shalt have no other gods before Me."

Thou holy and mighty God, who spoke these words to us; please let any satanic covenant of initiation forged against me consciously or unconsciously, be broken permanently by the power in the blood of Jesus, the Blood of Redemption, in Jesus name. Father God, please always deliver my dreams from any satanic evil foundation in the name of Jesus.

Matthew 15:13 reads:

"But He answered and said, every plant, which my heavenly Father hath not planted, shall be rooted up."

Everlasting Father, please let any stranger or moving objects programmed into my body by ancestral spirits, to defile my temple, be uprooted by Your fire in Jesus' name.

Father God, since my body is the temple of the Holy Spirit, please let any enemy attacking my body sexually while I was supposed to be sleeping and depositing evil things inside my body be uprooted by Your fire in Jesus' name. Let any satanic power, whether spiritual or human, challenging what Jesus stands for in my life and body be flushed away by the blood of Jesus and the fire of the Holy Ghost in the name of Jesus.

Isaiah 2:12 reads:
"For the day of the LORD of hosts shall be upon everyone that is proud and lofty; and upon every one that is lifted up; and he shall be brought low."
O holy Judge of this whole earth, please let my boastful enemies who are attacking Your plans for my life now receive Your righteous judgement and fail permanently in the mighty name of Jesus.

Isaiah 54:15 reads:
"Behold they shall surely gather together, but not by me: whosoever shall gather together against thee shall fall for thy sake."
O God of power and might, please let all my enemies, spiritual and physical, that gather against me by day and by night fall for my sake in the name of Jesus.

Jeremiah 39:18
"For I will surely deliver thee, and thou shalt not fall by the sword, but thy life shall be for a prey unto thee: because thou hast put thy trust in me, said the LORD."
From perils of the enemy, perils in the land, air, or sea, perils of the body, weather, economy, foundational

bondage, O most merciful God, please deliver me, so that I may live and do Your work in Jesus' name.

Jeremiah 20:11 reads:
"But the LORD is with me as a mighty terrible one: therefore my persecutors shall stumble, and they shall not prevail: they shall be greatly ashamed; for they shall not prosper: their everlasting confusion shall never be forgotten."
O Thou awesome God, mighty in battle, please delegate Your warrior angels to bring to utter confusion and failure to all the enemies of my soul in Jesus' name.

Psalm 18:44–45 reads:
"As soon as they hear of me, they shall obey me: the strangers shall submit themselves unto me. The strangers shall fade away, and be afraid out of their close places."
Plead the blood of Jesus 7 times, and pray: O Holy God of might and power, please let all spiritual strangers in my body and in my life be afraid and fade away from their closed places in Jesus' name.
O God, please let any evil stranger that followed me to this place in order to destroy me fail permanently in Jesus' name.

Prayer Against Spiritual Husband/Wife
2 Corinthians 6:15– 17 reads:
"And what concord hath Christ with Belial? or what part hath he that believeth with an infidel? And what agreement hath the temple of God with idols? for ye are

the temple of the living God, as God hath said, I will dwell in them, and walk in them; and I will be their GOD, and they shall be my people. Wherefore come out from among them, and be ye separate, saith the Lord, and touch not the unclean thing: and I will receive you." O Holy God of deliverance, please let any spiritual animal working to defile or destroy my body and my salvation be uprooted from my life forever in the name of Jesus. Let any association that will bring defilement into my life and as a result, make You, my God, to turn away from me be broken in Jesus' name.

Father Lord, let any unbroken covenant made consciously or unconsciously, whether by me or by my ancestors or relatives on my behalf be finally broken by the power in the blood of Jesus in Jesus' name. (Drum several times): Be broken by the blood of Jesus, in Jesus' name.

O Holy God, please put a wall of the blood of Jesus around me, so that any deposit in my body will be flushed out by the blood.

I loose myself from the enemy in Jesus' name. I am loosed from him/her in heaven in Jesus' name.

Prayer Against the General Enemy

Psalm 18:28 reads:

"For thou wilt light my candle: The LORD my God will enlighten my darkness."

O God, please let Your glory in my life overshadow and terminate the work of darkness, in Jesus' name. Let holiness overshadow sin in my life in the name of Jesus.

Psalm 18:47– 48 reads:
"It is God that avengeth me, and subdueth the people under me. He delivereth me from my enemies, yea, thou liftest me up above those that rise up against me; thou hast delivered me from the violent man."
O mighty God of war, the battle is Yours not mine. Please avenge me of all my unrepentant enemies in the name of Jesus.

In 1 John 3:8, it is written that for the reason of sin which the devil inflicted on man, the Son of God came into this world to destroy the works of the devil.
O God, please let all the work of the devil in my foundation be permanently destroyed in Jesus' name.

Psalm 91:13 reads:
"Thou shalt tread upon the lion and adder: the young lion and the dragon shalt thou trample under feet."
Merciful God, the eternal Source of all power, please as I spiritually tread upon the satanic and spiritual enemies, give me permanent victory over them in Jesus' name.

Psalm 55:2–3 reads:
"Attend unto me, and hear me: I mourn in my complaint, and make a noise; Because of the voice of the enemy, because of the oppression of the wicked, for they cast iniquity upon me, and in wrath they hate me."
Jehovah Nisi, my great Banner, please speak failure to the aggressive attacks of the wicked in my life. O, let

their wickedness come to an end suddenly in the name of Jesus.

Exodus 9:1, 15 reads:
"Then the LORD said unto Moses, Go in unto Pharaoh, and tell him, Thus saith the LORD God of the Hebrews, Let my people go, that they may serve me. ...
"For now I will stretch out my hand, that I may smite thee and thy people with pestilence".
O God of Abraham, Isaac, and Jacob, please let the ancestral spirits still enraged and are continuously laying snares, attacking us day and night, because my family and I are redeemed by the blood of Jesus Christ, be seriously challenged by Your fire, defeated, and chased away permanently in the name of Jesus.

James 4:7 reads:
"Submit yourselves therefore to God. Resist the devil, and he will flee from you."
Father Lord, please give me the grace to submit to You in order to be able to resist my enemies, so that they can be compelled to flee from me in Jesus' name.
Please God, do not allow these enemies to constitute a hindrance to my progress anymore in Jesus' name.

2 Samuel 15:31b reads:
"And David said, O LORD, I pray thee, turn the counsel of Ahithophel into foolishness."
Isaiah 8:10 reads:

"Take counsel together, and it shall come to nought; speak the word, and it shall not stand: for God is with us."

My Holy Father and my God, I plead with You, please let all the many counsels and meetings of the enemies against me and my family always turn to nothing in Jesus' name.

Psalm 27:12 reads:

"Deliver me not over unto the will of mine enemies; for false witnesses are risen up against me, and such as breathe out cruelty."

O God, please let all the satanic accusations of my enemies against me day and night be directed back to where they came from in the name of Jesus.

Matthew 15:13 reads:

"But he answered and said, Every plant, which my heavenly Father hath not planted, shall be rooted up."

My Father, my Father, my Father; I cry out to You today in agony and distress, and say, please let any tree of spiritual animals or demons responsible for different evils which You did not plant in my body or life be now rooted out permanently, in the name of Jesus.

2 Corinthians. 5:17 reads:

"Therefore if any man be in Christ, he is a new creature: old things are passed away, behold all things are become new."

O God of miracles, signs, and wonders, Thou Holy God, mighty in battle, who turns the plans of our enemies upside down, please let any spiritual enemy always trying to forge spiritual marriage in my dreams and in life be permanently defeated and driven away in the mighty name of Jesus.

1 Corinthians 16:9 reads:
"For a great door and effectual is opened unto me, and there are many adversaries."
O God, please let all hindrances, oppositions, and obstructions mounted against me spiritually and physically be dismantled by Your fire in the name of Jesus.

Acts 23:21 reads:
"But do not thou yield unto them: for there lie in wait for him of them more than forty men, which have bound themselves with an oath, that they will neither eat nor drink till they have killed him: and now are they ready, looking for a promise from thee."
Jehovah Nisi, my great Warrior, please let any enemy that took a covenant against my salvation and my life be exceedingly disappointed, defeated, and permanently driven away in the name of Jesus.
Confess this scripture several times: I shall not die, but live to declare and do the work of God in the land of the living in Jesus' name.

Psalm 27:2 reads:

"When the wicked, even mine enemies and my foes, came upon me to eat up my flesh, they stumbled and fell."

My Holy God and my Shield, please let all the enemies that came to eat up my destiny and my salvation stumble and fall permanently in the name of Jesus.

Colossians 2:14–15 reads:

"Blotting out the handwriting of ordinances that was against us, which was contrary to us, and took it out of the way, nailing it to his cross; and having spoiled principalities and powers, he made a shew of them openly, triumphing over them in it."

O God, please let any attempt by our enemies to rise above this position which You placed them, under us, be rejected with severe torment, affliction, and permanent subjection in the name of Jesus.

John 1:5 reads:

"And the light shineth in darkness; and the darkness comprehended it not."

O Holy God of my light and salvation, please let every area of darkness in my life be chalenged by fire and be illuminated forever by Your light in the name of Jesus.

Revelation 3:7b reads:

"He that opens, and no man shuts; and shuts, and no man opens".

O Holy God who opens and no one shuts; shuts and no one opens, please let any door way which You have opened in my life and enemy is trynd to padlock, be set ablaze by Your fire and be melted in Jesus' name.

Psalm 35:1 reads:
"Plead my cause, O LORD, with them that strive with me: fight against them that fight against me."
Holy Father, God, please use Your right hand of fire and power to restrain the continuous attacks of the enemy in my life in the name of Jesus.

Psalm 35:7 reads:
"For without cause have they hid for me their net in a pit, which without cause they have digged for my soul."
O Holy God, the Giver of life, please let me not die, but live to declare and do Your work in the land of the living in the name of Jesus.
Let that enemy that planned my death see me alive, prospering in health and wealth, just as my soul prospers, in the name of Jesus.

Psalm 35:4 reads:
"Let them be confounded and put to shame that seek after my soul; let them be turned back and brought to confusion that devise my hurt."
O God, my Fortress, You are a God of war. Please fight my battles for me because whatever You start, You finish (Philippians 1:6).

Drum several times: Holy Father, God, please fight my battles for me in the name of Jesus.

Ecclesiastes 10:8 reads:
"He that diggeth a pit shall fall into it; and whoso breaketh a hedge, a serpent shall bite him."
O God, my Banner, please forgive me if I have opened a way for Satan through sin. Let every doorway through which I am receiving attacks be permanently shut in the name of Jesus.

Psalm 35:10 reads:
"All thy bones shall say LORD, who is like unto Thee, which delivers the poor from him that is too strong for him, yea, the poor and the needy from him that spoileth them."
My Father and my God, Your strength is made perfect in weakness. Please do not let my unrepentant enemies triumph over me in the name of Jesus.
O God, please let all the gathering of my enemies be driven away by Your fire in Jesus' name.

Psalm 35:19–23:
"Let not them that are mine enemies wrongfully rejoice over me: neither let them wink with the eye that hate me without a cause. For they speak not peace: but they devise deceitful matters against them that are quiet in the land. Yea, they opened their mouth wide against me, and said, Aha aha, our eye hath seen it."

Holy God, You foresee the end from the beginning, if the enemies who are in hot pursuit of my life genuinely repent, please forgive them. If they refuse to repent and are dead bent on destroying me, let Your word judge them, and let Your will be perfected in them in Jesus' name.

Psalm 46:6, 9–10 reads:
"The heathen raged, the kingdoms were moved: he uttered his voice, the earth melted."
Verses 9 and 10 read:
"He maketh wars to cease unto the end of the earth; he breaketh the bow, and cutteth the spear in sunder; he burneth the chariot in the fire. Be still, and know that I am God: I will be exalted among the heathen, I will be exalted in the earth."
O Holy God, mighty in battle, the One whose name alone is Jehovah, please speak silence and defeat into the rage and attacks of my enemies in the name of Jesus.
Drum several times: Please speak silence and defeat into the camp of my enemies in the name of Jesus

Psalm 55:12–14 reads:
"For it was not an enemy that reproached me; then I could have borne it: neither was it he that hated me that did magnify himself against me; then I would have hid myself from him: but it was thou, a man mine equal, my guide, and mine acquaintance."
Thou God of mercy and compassion, please minister

repentance to the heart of my enemy, but do not allow him to overcome me, in Jesus' name. When you dream of death, make the following scriptural declarations, and pray the prayer next to them.

Psalm 118:17 reads:
"I shall not die, but live, and declare the works of the LORD" in the name of Jesus.
Romans 8:2 reads:
"For the law of the Spirit of life in Christ Jesus hath made me free from the law of sin and death."
Romans 8:11 reads:
"But if the Spirit of Him that raised up Jesus from the dead dwell in you, he that raised up Christ from the dead shall also quicken your mortal bodies by his Spirit that dwelleth in you."
O Holy Spirit of the living God, please quicken my mortal body to the glory of God in Jesus' name.
Jehovah God, the Giver of life and health, please let any spiritual burial fashioned against me be reversed by the blood of Jesus in Jesus' name.
O God, please cancel any threat of death to my life in Jesus' name.

Philippians 2:10 reads:
"That at the name of Jesus every knee should bow, of things in heaven, and things in earth, and things under the earth."
O God, please let every knee of witchcraft attack,

marine spirit attacks, foundational attacks, occultism, disobedience, obstructions, demonic delays, cobwebs, spiritual attacks, dream attacks, sexual attacks, spiritual marriage attack, and eating in the dream, bow permanently at the name of Jesus. Pick any one pertaining to you, and drum the prayer several times.

Mark 6:50b reads:
"Be of good cheer: it is I; be not afraid."
Psalm 46:10 reads:
"Be still, and know that I am GOD: I will be exalted among the heathen, I will be exalted in the earth."
Make the following declaration:
You, menacing, ever threatening, and boastful attacks of my spiritual and physical foundational enemies against my life, progress, and family, be still and know that my God is a God of war. You, my trembling heart, though still trusting in the Lord, be of good cheer. The Lord is in control. He is the same God who suddenly brought the boastful Goliath dead flat on the ground; the same God who parted the Red Sea for the Israelites to escape and drowned the proud, boastful, and unbelieving Egyptians and their horses in the same sea; the same God who pulled down the walls of Jericho with songs and praises made to Him, He is still the same God who put a hook in the nose of the threatening King of Assyria (when he came to annihilate Judah) and turned him backwards by the way he came. The One who sent one angel to slay a hundred and eighty-five thousand Assyrians in one night.

My Holy Father and my Warrior, You are the same yesterday, today, and forever. Please do for me what You did for the Israelites in trouble, in the mighty name of Jesus. Let the glory be all Yours in Jesus' name.

Thank You Holy God, for answered prayers.

Galatians 6:7– 8 reads:

"Be not deceived; GOD is not mocked; for whatsoever a man soweth, that shall he also reap. For he that soweth to his flesh shall of the flesh reap corruption; but he that soweth to the Spirit shall of the Spirit reap life everlasting."

Holy Father, God, please minister the spirit of genuine repentance to those enemies who are sowing evil seeds in my life, so that they do not perish in their ungodly acts in Jesus' name (Psalm 1:6).

Isaiah 49:26 reads:

"And I will feed them that oppress thee with their own flesh; and they shall be drunken with their own blood, as with sweet wine: and all flesh shall know that I the LORD am thy Saviour and thy Redeemer, the mighty One of Jacob."

Jehovah Elohim, my eternal Creator, please make my enemies to fight against themselves in Jesus' name.

Let any part of my body or life which witches and wizards have swallowed spiritually or buried on the ground be vomited or exhumed in the name of Jesus.

O God, please render all my enemies powerless in Jesus' name.

Revelation 3:7 reads:

"And to the angel of the Church in Philadelphia write; These things saith he that is holy, he that is true, he that hath the key of David, he that openeth, and no man shutteth; and shutteth, and no man openeth."

O God, be thou my strength in the time of trouble; push me forward with Your mighty hand of fire and power in the name of Jesus.

Everlasting Father, who is able to do exceeding abundantly above all that we ask or think, please let the enemy that is always trying to shut the door that You opened in my life receive automatic punishment from You in the name of Jesus.

Drum several times: Let them receive automatic punishment in the name of Jesus. Push me forward with Your fire in the name of Jesus.

O Holy Lord, please let all the spiritual padlocks that the enemy is using to padlock my doors be melted by Your fire in the name of Jesus.

Psalm 144:10 reads:

"It is He that giveth salvation unto kings: who delivereth David his servant from the hurtful sword."

Father, God, please let all the spiritual and physical enemies who are using satanic force to pull me away from my salvation receive the fire of resistance in the name of Jesus.

Psalm 37:17 reads:

"For the arms of the wicked shall be broken: but the LORD upholdeth the righteous."

O God, my strong Tower, please let all those enemies who preoccupy themselves with trying to destroy all the good things that You bring into my life receive serious resistance from Your fire in the name of Jesus.

Luke 10:19 reads:

'Behold I give unto you power to tread on serpents and scorpions, and over all the power of the enemy: and nothing shall by any means hurt you."

O God, the Strength of my life, please let these Your words not return back to You but accomplish what they are purposed to accomplish in this prayer in Jesus' name. O covenant-keeping God, please empower me to exercise adequate faith in Your power to overcome attacks, afflictions, sufferings, and confrontations for me, in the mighty name of Jesus.

Number 23:8 reads:

"How shall I curse whom God hath not cursed? or how shall I defy whom the Lord hath not defied?"

Galatians 3:13– 14 reads:

"Christ hath redeemed us from the curse of the law, being made a curse for us: for it is written, Cursed is anyone that hangeth on a tree: That the blessing of Abraham might come on the Gentiles through Jesus Christ; that we might receive the promise of the spirit through faith." My eternal Redeemer, since the curse that has no justification shall not stand, please let any curse ever put on me a believer and my family be broken by the blood of Jesus that was shed for its destruction in the name of Jesus.

Acts 1:8 reads:
"But you shall receive power, after that the Holy Ghost is come upon you: and ye shall be witnesses unto me both in Jerusalem, and in all Judea, and in Samaria, and unto the uttermost part of the earth."
O Holy God of might and power, please give me the power and the resources to support and carry the gospel to the farthest parts of this world in the name of Jesus.
Let me fight to win all souls for You in the name of Jesus.

John 11:44 reads:
"And he that was dead came forth, bound hand and foot with grave clothes, and his face was bound about with a napkin. Jesus said unto them, loose him and let him go."
Thou Giver of life and health, the great Deliverer, please let anywhere that I have been bound or tied in the spirit world receive Your power and fire, and set me free, in the name of Jesus.

Exodus 20:3 reads:
"Thou shalt have no other gods before me."
O Thou the only true God, please let any satanic

covenant of initiation forged against me consciously or unconsciously be broken by the power in the blood of Jesus in Jesus' name.

Let any satanic power masquerading as You, my God, in my spiritual and physical life be permanently driven away by Your whirlwind in the mighty name of Jesus.

Isaiah 8:10 reads:

"Take counsel together and it shall come to nothing; speak the word and it shall not stand for God is with us."

O God, please turn all the evil counsels of my enemies to confusion, and let their evil pronouncements not stand in Jesus' name.

Psalm 50:15 reads:

"And call upon me in the day of trouble I will deliver thee, and thou shalt glorify me."

O God, please deliver me from my strong enemies who hate me, for they are too strong for me in Jesus' name. Let Your power, as of old, minister deliverance to me in Jesus' name.

Galatians 3:13 reads:

"Christ hath redeemed us from the curse of the law, being made a curse for us: for it is written, Cursed is every one that hangeth on a tree."

O God, please let all the generational curses issued against my family be broken by Thy power in the blood of Jesus in the name of Jesus.

Exodus 20:2 reads:

"I am the LORD thy God, which have brought thee out of the land of Egypt, out of the house of bondage."

Holy God, who led the Israelites out of Egypt, please lead me out of the incessant attacks of my ancestral and foundational enemies in the name of Jesus.

Matthew 18:18 reads:

"Verily I say unto you, Whatsoever ye shall bind on earth shall be bound in heaven: and whatsoever ye shall loose on earth shall be loosed in heaven."

Father, in the name of Jesus, I loose every part of my body, my life, my ministry, family, finances, possessions, health, and prosperity from every occult attacks and witchcraft bondage in Jesus' name (demonstrate as you pray).

I repossess all my ... in the name of Jesus.

Proverbs 19:21 reads:

"There are many devices in a man's heart, nevertheless the counsel of the LORD, that shall stand."

O Holy God, my strong Tower, please let Your counsel always prevail over the evil devices of all my enemies in Jesus' name.

Romans 8:26–27 reads:

"Likewise the Spirit also helpeth our infirmities: for we know not what we should pray for as we ought: but the Spirit itself maketh intercession for us with groanings which cannot be uttered.

And he that searcheth the hearts knoweth what is in the mind of the Spirit, because he maketh intercession for the saints according to the will of God."

Blessed Holy Spirit of the living God, please when my case gets tough, intercede for me in the language which only You can understand in Jesus' name.

Romans 8:31 reads:

"What shall we then say to these things? If God be for us, who can be against us?"

O Holy God, my strong Tower, because You are for me, please do not allow any arrow to hit me or any member of my family in Jesus' name.

Please give me the empowerment to labour righteously for You and to withstand any attack in Jesus' name.

Jeremiah 20:11 reads:

"But the LORD is with me as a mighty terrible one: therefore my persecutors shall stumble, and they shall not prevail: they shall be greatly ashamed, for they shall not prosper: their everlasting confusion shall never be forgotten."

Almighty God, my Strength and Redeemer, please release the spirit of confusion on every gathering of my enemies; let them always fail by Your power in the name of Jesus

1 Corinthians 10:13 reads:

"There hath no temptation taken you, but such as is common to man: but God is faithful, who will not suffer you to be tempted above that ye are able: but will with the temptation, also make a way to escape, that ye may be able to bear it."

O able Father of all power and mercies, please give me the power to overcome all temptations that will arise in my life in Jesus' name. May I never succumb to any of them in the name of Jesus.

Psalm 22:10–12 reads:

"I was cast upon thee from the womb: thou art my God from my mother's belly. Be not far from me; for trouble is near; for there is none to help. … Strong bulls of Bashan have beset me round."

My God, my God, You created me in Your own image, gave me a destiny, and have protected me all this while; please empower me to always walk away from enemy attacks, confidently and victoriously, and also, to glorify You in the name of Jesus.

2 Timothy 4:18 reads:

"And the Lord shall deliver me from every evil work, and will preserve me unto his heavenly kingdom: to whom be glory forever and ever. Amen."

My holy Deliverer and my God, please let Your mighty hand of mercy and deliverance continue to uphold me all the days of my life, so that I may glorify You in Jesus' name.

Psalm 91:11–12 reads:

"For he shall give his angels charge over thee, to keep thee in all thy ways. They shall bear thee up in their hands, lest thou dash thy foot against a stone."

O God, my Fortress, please let Your angels always encamp around me to deliver me at every point of attack and to preserve me blameless for the Kingdom in the name of Jesus.

Psalm 91:5–6. reads:

"Thou shalt not be afraid for the terror by night; nor for the arrow that flieth by day;

Nor for the pestilence that walketh in darkness; nor for the destruction that wasteth at noonday."

Surely, Holy God, there are terrors and pestilences in the night and arrows and destruction in the day. Please let Your hand of mercy and protection continue to shield me and my family from them. Let us live to be eternally grateful to You in Jesus' name.

Psalm 23:4 reads:

"Yea, though I walk through the valley of the shadow of death, I will fear no evil: for thou art with me; thy rod and thy staff, they comfort me."

No matter the severity of the suffering and deprivation, no matter the terminal nature of the sickness, no matter the uncertainty of the financial situation, Thy faithfulness, O God, abideth for ever. Help us to abide even on a greater faith; so that Your miraculous hand can guide us out of it all in Jesus' name.

Zechariah 5:3–5 reads:
"Then said he unto me, This is the curse that goeth forth over the face of the whole earth: for every one that stealeth shall be cut off as on this side according to it; and everyone that sweareth shall be cut off as on that side according to it.

"I will bring it forth, saith the LORD of Hosts, and it shall enter into the house of the thief, and into the house of him that sweareth falsely by my name, and it shall remain in the midst of his house, and shall consume it with the timber thereof and the stores thereof."

Everlasting Father, merciful, loving, and forgiving, please I plead with You in the name of Your beloved Son Jesus Christ, that if there have been occasions in my past where I or my ancestors have done anything that attracted one curse or another into the life of the family that You will have mercy and forgive. I am truly sorry and truly repent with my whole heart in Jesus' name.

Psalm 27:12 reads:
"Deliver me not over unto the will of mine enemies: for false witnesses are risen up against me, and such as breathe out cruelty."

Holy Father, God of war, behold my foundational enemies. Behold how they invade my house day and night, planning to steal, kill, and destroy. But it is written in John 10:10 that "I am come that they might have life, and that they might have it more abundantly."

It is also written in 2 Corinthians 5:17 that "Therefore, if any man be in Christ, he is a new creature: old things are passed away; behold, all things are become new."

Please holy covenant-keeping God, force these unrepentant spiritual enemies and their physical agents to accept defeat and to flee from us permanently in the name of Jesus. Let them return the way they came, O Holy God, and not come back to my family again in the name of Jesus.

Isaiah 27:4 reads:

"Fury is not in me: who would set the briers and thorns against me in battle? I would go through them, I would burn them together."

Victorious Warrior, mighty in battle, please let any power of the enemy contending with Your power in my life receive reprimand and be driven away permanently in the name of Jesus.

My High Priest and my Judge, please let any power resisting Your progress in my life receive Your immediate judgement in the name of Jesus. Let their failures be sudden and permanent in the name of Jesus.

Matthew 4:10 reads:

"Thou shalt worship the LORD thy God, and him only shalt thou serve."

My Holy God and my Lord, my Creator and Father of our Lord Jesus Christ, please let any power masquerading as You; my God, Jesus Christ, the Holy Spirit, or Your angels in my life; be disgraced, defeated, and uprooted in the name of Jesus.

Then declare: I shall worship the holy Lord, my God, Him only shall I serve. I refuse to have any other God besides Him. Also, teach your children to pray this prayer every day. This may help to absolve you from the sin of unconscious idolatry or at least win the sympathy of God against being held responsible for what you were ignorant of.

You must try to pray this prayer throughout your life time. You can hardly predict when there is an urgent need for it.

Psalm 91:9 reads:

"Because thou hast made the LORD, which is my refuge, even the Most High, thy habitation, there shall no evil befall thee, neither shall any plague come nigh thy dwelling."

Holy God, my Shield and my Defender, please let any satanic arrow targeted at me, my place of habitation, miss its target and be destroyed by Your fire in Jesus' name.

You are advised to make this crucial intercession every day. As you pray for others, God can answer your prayers also.

Psalm 37:14 reads:

"The wicked have drawn out the sword, and have bent their bow, to cast down the poor and needy, and to slay such as be of upright conversation."

O Holy Lord of hosts, mighty in battle, please let all those who Satan has planned to terminate their lives today through different satanic means of destruction be delivered for the sake of the shed blood on the Cross. Have mercy and forgive their sins. Grant them more years, so that they can be led to salvation and prepare for heaven in the name of Jesus.

Make the Following Confessions:

We worship the holy Lord, our God, Him only do we serve. We have no other God besides Him. Our enemies chose Satan and multiplied their sorrows. Their drink offering of blood, we shall not offer neither take up the name of Satan in our lips.

Therefore, you, my enemies, you will not offer my blood or that of my family to Satan because Jesus, our Redeemer, died and paid our price with the shed blood on the Cross. I stand on the scripture in Rom 8:2 which states that "The law of the Spirit of Life in Christ Jesus has delivered us from the law of sin and death" Also in John 10:10, to declare that you will no longer steal, kill, destroy, or remain in my house anymore. It is also written in Psalm 27:2 that, "When the wicked, even mine enemies and my foes, came upon me to eat up my flesh, they stumbled and fell."

So it shall happen to you, my enemies, in the name of Jesus. No weapon you fashion against me shall prosper, and God will disappoint all your evil devices against me, so that you cannot perform your evil enterprise. The Lord is the Strength of my live, and I condemn every tongue you raise up against me in judgement. If you speak the Word, it will not stand; if you take counsel together, it will come to nothing. God will fight for me, and I shall hold my peace in Jesus' name.

Holy Father God, You have defeated my enemies for me so far, please perfect that defeat to Your eternal glory in Jesus' name.

Psalm 18:13–14 reads:

"The LORD also thundered in the heavens, and the Highest gave his voice; hail stones and coals of fire. Yea, he sent out his arrows, and scattered them; and he shot out lightnings, and discomfited them."

O Holy God of war who has never failed, please perfect Your victory over our enemies, and force them to accept defeat and to flee from us in Jesus' name.

O Holy Judge of the whole world, please let me witness the extreme confusion, disappointment, and permanent failure of all those enemies who are trying to terminate Your ministry in my life in the name of Jesus.

Psalm 91:9–10 reads:

"Because thou hast made the LORD, which is my refuge, even the most High, thy habitation: there shall no evil befall thee, neither shall any plague come nigh thy dwelling."

Eternal Deliverer, my Fortress and Strength, because I

have made You, our Refuge and Habitation, please let every satanic arrow fired against me always miss their target and fail permanently in the name of Jesus.

Lamentations 3:22 reads:
"It is of the LORD'S mercies that we are not consumed, because his compassions fail not."
O merciful God of compassion, please give to all our human enemies the spirit of genuine repentance in the name of Jesus.
O Holy God of war, please let any enemy who has refused to stop attacking the work which You have already completed, spiritually, in my life be automatically chased away permanently by the heat of Your fire in the name of Jesus.

Isaiah 28:18 reads:
"And your covenant with death shall be disannulled, and your agreement with hell shall not stand".
Father of all truth, please let all those who plan to terminate other people's lives always fail in the name of Jesus.

1 Peter 4:7 reads:
"But the end of all things is at hand: be ye therefore sober, and watch unto prayer."
Everlasting Father, please keep me spiritually awake in my dreams, so that I can withstand and defeat, by Your power, the attacks of the spiritual masquerades, and the

other enemies in my dreams in Jesus' name.

Luke 16:26 reads:

"And beside all these, between us and you, there is a great gulf fixed so that they which will pass from hence to you cannot; neither can they pass to us, that would come from thence."

Satan, according to the words of Father Abraham to the rich man, the blood of Jesus has already created a great gulf between us, the redeemed, and you. No weapon you fashioned against us shall prosper, and all your arrows will be returned back to you, the sender, in the name of Jesus.

End this section by proclaiming the power of God at work in your life. Tell God that you are fully aware of the fact that He can achieve all victories in your life to His eternal glory, and that there is no limit to His power in the name of Jesus. Thank Him for answered prayer.

Chapter 8

DREAMS

Dreams are the theatre where spiritual enemies play out their evil parts. It is the location where human progress and endeavours can be turned upside down. If you can defeat the enemy in the dream through the help of God, you can do so in real life. Prayers about dreams should be taken very seriously. Do as much as you can of the praise worship, and forgiveness prayers first before these prayers.

Prayers
I thank You, Holy God, because this whole earth including my dream life belong to You; the world and all that lives in it belong to You. For You made my dreams part of my life and established it for Your operations in my sleep. Lift up your heads, O ye gates of my dreams; and be ye lifted up, ye ancient doors of my dreams; and the Holy God of glory and miracles will come in. (paraphrase)
Plead the blood of Jesus on your dreams seven (7) times, and then pray as follows;
Holy Father, I thank You for Your hand of protection

and mercy placed on my dreams. May my dreams always glorify You in Jesus' name. Do not let me associate with the dead in my dreams in Jesus' name.

O God, let no weapon of the enemy fashioned against me in the dream and in life ever prosper in the mighty name of Jesus.

Psalm 144:1–2 reads:

"Blessed be the LORD my strength, which teacheth my hands to war, and my fingers to fight; my high tower and my deliverer, … Who subdueth my people under me."

Immortal Redeemer, please use me as Your battle axe to fight and defeat all my enemies in the dream every day until they are defeated permanently in Jesus' name.

O God, please empower me always to assume the offensive over my enemies in the dream, and always deliver me from them in the name of Jesus.

Holy Father of all mercies, please electrify my dreams with Your fire whenever the enemy tries to attack me in the name of Jesus.

Jeremiah 30:16 reads:

"Therefore all they that devour thee shall be devoured; and all thine adversaries every one of them, shall go into captivity, and they that spoil thee shall be a spoil, and all that prey upon thee will I give for a prey."

My Holy Father and my God, please let everything that I have lost to devourers in my dream, which You consider still right for me, be recovered to me full fold, and may these devourers also be devoured in Jesus' name.

O Holy God of all righteousness, please let any weapon of financial theft fashioned against me in the dream be reversed by the power in the blood of Jesus, in Jesus' name.

Matthew 11:12 reads:
"And from the days of John the Baptist until now the kingdom of heaven suffereth violence, and the violent take it by force."
O Holy God of power and might, please let Your force of power enforce Your will in my dreams and in my life forever in Jesus' name.

O Holy God of power, wherever the enemy has forcefully installed hindrances against Your will and purposes in my dream, please let them be uprooted permanently in Jesus' name. I have received salvation from Christ, and the enemy cannot force me against my will to renounce it in the dream in Jesus' name. Jesus has opened the door of eternal life for me, and no power can shut it. I refuse to be manipulated especially in my dreams against the will of God for my life in the name of Jesus.

1 Corinthians 10:21 reads:
"Ye cannot drink the cup of the LORD, and the cup of devils: ye cannot be partakers of the Lord's table, and of the table of devils."
O God, please let any spiritual enemy that comes to feed me in the dream always receive receive the challenge of Your angels in the Name of Jesus.

2 Corinthians 6:16–17 reads:

"And what agreement hath the temple of God with idols? For ye are the temple of the living God; as God hath said, I will dwell in them, and walk in them; and I will be their God, and they shall be my people. Wherefore come out from among them, and be ye separate, saith the LORD and touch not the unclean thing: and I will receive you." Father of all truth, Holy Lord God, please let all spiritual and physical enemies forging spiritual marriages, initiations, and projecting demons as children into my dreams receive torment and permanent failure in Jesus' name.

O Holy God, my Deliverer, please let any spiritual enemy masquerading as a husband, wife, mother, or child in my dreams be chased away permanently by Your fire and pain in the name of Jesus.

John 1:5 reads:

"And the light shineth in darkness, and the darkness comprehended it not."

John 9:5 reads:

"As long as I am in the world, I am the light of the world." Father Lord, because I worship You the Father and Creator of light, please let every spirit of darkness operating in my dreams and in my life be chased away permanently by Your light in Jesus' name. Let not darkness comprehend light in my dream and life in Jesus' name.

1 Corinthians 16:9 reads:

"For a great door and effectual is opened unto me, and there are many adversaries."

Father Lord, You open a door and no power can shut it because Your right hand has done it, and no power can reverse it. Please let any enemy that wants to challenge Your power by trying to shut any door You open in my dreams and in my life fail suddenly and permanently in Jesus' name.

Psalm 18:38–39 reads:

"I have wounded them that they were not able to rise: they are fallen under my feet. For thou hast girded me with strength unto the battle: thou hast subdued under me those that rose up against me."

O Holy God, my only strength, please empower me to always assume the offensive against my enemies in the dream. Let Your angels encamp around me in my dreams to scatter and permanently defeat all the gatherings of the enemy in Jesus' name.

Philippians 4:13 reads:

"I can do all things through Christ which strengtheneth me."

Father God, please give me the enablement to never lose any battle in the dreams, in the name of Jesus. Anoint me to receive permanent victory in my dreams in Jesus' name.

Revelations 3:8 reads:

"I know thy works: behold I have set before thee an open door, and no man can shut it."

O God, please let all the spiritual padlocks which the enemy uses to padlock the doors of Your purpose and progress in my dream be reversed and used to padlock their own evil plans and progress in the name of Jesus.

Psalm 23:5a reads:

"Thou preparest a table before me in the presence of my enemies".

Everlasting Father of glory, just as in 2 Kings 7:2, Elisha told the doubting lord on whose hand the king leaned that he would see a measure of fine flour being sold for a shekel, and two measures of barley for a shekel, but that he would not eat of it: so let my enemies, both spiritual and human in the dream, see the table that You will prepare for me in their presence, but please let them not devour or touch it, both in the dream and life, in the name of Jesus.

The high and mighty God, Thou great Creator, please in the name of Your Son Jesus Christ, let that hand of power and mercy that performed all these miracles; that turned all the waters in Egypt into blood; that opened the ground and it swallowed 250 family members; that commanded the storm to be still and the disciples were relieved; that wiped off the Amalekites from the surface of the earth, speak 'time up' to my spiritual and physical enemies messing up my dreams. Let it quench the rage of these enemies in my dreams, in the name of Jesus.

O God please let all the demonic actors and actresses operating in my dreams be rooted out permanently in the name of Jesus.

Ecclesiastes 5:7 reads:

"For in the multitude of dreams and many words there are also diverse vanities: but fear thou God."

O God, please let every demonic interaction between my head and wicked spirits in my dreams be cancelled and wiped off by the blood of Jesus in Jesus' name. O Holy God, please give me the power to maintain spiritual discipline and obedience to Your word in my dreams in the name of Jesus. Holy Spirit please always stir up my consciousness in the dream, in the Name of Jesus

O Holy God, please do a new thing in my dreams today in the name of Jesus.

Matthew 15:13 reads:

"Every plant, which my heavenly Father hath not planted, shall be rooted out."

O God, please let all spiritual enemies masquerading as husband, mother, wife or children in my dream be permanently uprooted from my dreams, in the name of Jesus.

Psalm 34:21 reads:

"Evil shall slay the wicked: and they that hate the righteous shall be desolate."

O Holy God, the Creator, Owner, and Controller of my

dreams, please let all occults, wizards and witches, evil foundation, manipulating my dreams be permanently uprooted from my dreams in the name of Jesus. Numbers 23:23 reads: (Personalise this scripture as you pray.)

Numbers 23:23 reads:

"Surely there is no enchantment against Jacob, neither is there any divination against Israel: according to this time it shall be said of Jacob and of Israel, what hath God wrought."

O God, please let all the spiritual enemies, including their human agents, trying to alter the destiny of God in my dreams through bewitchment, spells, charms, enchantments, spells, hypnosis, and sexual incantations, etc., receive Your immediate judgement and punishment in the name of Jesus.

I bind every spirit of bewitchment, spell, charms, enchantments, jinxes, hexes, hypnotic incantations, operating in my dreams in Jesus' name. I cast them away forever, back to where they came from in the name of Jesus.

O God, please do not let me be manipulated to act in a manner which I am not supposed to act in the dream in the name of Jesus.

Daniel 2:22 reads:

"He revealeth the deep and secret things: he knoweth what is in the darkness, and the light dwelleth with him."

O Holy God of all truth and light, please reveal to me

the secrets of my enemy's powers and operations in the dreams in the name of Jesus.

O God to whom power belongs, please bestow on me the necessary spiritual insight, alertness, and discernment in my dreams in the name of Jesus.

Proverbs 4:16 reads:

"For they sleep not, except they have done mischief, and their sleep is taken away, unless they cause some to fall."

O Holy God, the Lord of hosts, please keep me spiritually awake in my sleep, so that I can recognize the spiritual masquerading of my enemies in the dreams and their operations; and, by Your power, combat them successfully in the name of Jesus.

O Holy God of battle, please challenge my dreams with the blood of Jesus and the fire of the Holy Ghost, in Jesus' name.

Job 20:8 reads:

"He shall fly away as a dream, and shall not be found: yea, he shall be chased away as a vision of the night."

O Holy God, please keep me in remembrance of all the dreams I had in the night, so that I can know what to pray against when I wake up, in the name of Jesus. Let all the satanic dreams that I had be chased away as a vision of the night, in Jesus Name.

Daniel 1:17b reads:

"And Daniel had understanding in all visions and dreams."

O God to whom wisdom and knowledge belong, please give me understanding of all my visions and dreams, so that I can grow in knowledge through Your training in my dreams in the name of Jesus.

O Holy God of power and might, please empower me to successfully resist the enemy and everything that he tries to do in my dreams in the name of Jesus.

Joel 2:28 reads:

"And it shall come to pass afterward, that I will pour out my spirit upon all flesh: and your sons and your daughters shall prophesy, your old men shall dream dreams, your young men shall see visions."

Holy God, the Creator of knowledge, please let all my dreams come from You. Empower me never to miss their right interpretations, in the name of Jesus.

O Holy God the strength of my life, please grant me the power to recover all the grounds that I lost in my dreams, in the name of Jesus.

Isaiah 26:3 reads:

"Thou wilt keep him in perfect peace, whose mind is stayed on thee: because he trusted in thee."

O Holy God of peace, please behold the rage and attack of my enemies in the dream. Protect and deliver me from them. Keep me in perfect peace, for I trust in You in the name of Jesus.

Father Lord, please anoint my head and my heart to reject every manipulation of the enemy in the dream and in life in Jesus' name. Train my mind, O God, to always focus on You in Jesus' name.

Luke 22:46 reads:
"And said unto them, why sleep ye? rise and pray, lest ye enter into temptation."
Father Lord, please keep me spiritually awake in my dreams, and empower me to successfully challenge and defeat the masquerading of my enemies in the dream, in the name of Jesus.

Matthew 13:25 reads:
"But while men slept, his enemies came and sowed tares among the wheat and went his way."
O God of power and truth, please let all the satanic projections that the enemy is sending to my dreams be uprooted and returned back in Jesus' name.
Let no weapon of bewitchment fashioned against my behaviour in the dream ever prosper, in the name of Jesus.

Isaiah 28:16 reads:
"Therefore thus said the Lord GOD, Behold, I lay in Zion for a foundation a stone, a tried stone, a precious corner stone a sure foundation".
O God, my Deliverer and the Creator of my dreams, please deliver my dreams from any evil foundation in the name of Jesus.
Holy God, please let my dreams be laid on the foundation of the Lord Jesus Christ and be evacuated of

all foundational enemies in the name of Jesus.

Holy God, please soak my dreams in the blood of Jesus in Jesus' name.

Job 33:14–16 reads:

"For God speaketh once, yea twice, yet man perceiveth it not. In a dream, in a vision of the night, when deep sleep falleth upon men, in slumbering upon the bed; then he openeth the ears of men, and sealeth their instruction."

By Your power and might, O God, please speak secret and knowledgeable things to me in the dream that will enhance Your power, and deliver me from my enemies in the dream in the name of Jesus.

I reject the enemy's spirit of deceit and masquerading in my dreams in the name of Jesus. I bind the spirit of ignorance and forgetfulness, and cast them away from my dreams and life in the name of Jesus.

O Holy God, please bathe my dreams with the blood of Jesus in Jesus' name.

Jeremiah 23:28 reads:

"The prophet that hath a dream, let him tell a dream; and he that hath my word, let him speak my word faithfully. What is the chaff to the wheat? saith the LORD."

Most merciful God, please forgive and deliver me from the sin of distorting Your word in the interpretation of my dreams and messages in the name of Jesus. Please put the right fear of You in my life, so that I can be more careful and precise in giving any message from You in the name of Jesus.

Psalm 18:44–45 reads:

"As soon as they hear of me, they shall obey me: the strangers shall submit themselves unto me. The strangers shall fade away, and be afraid out of their closed places."

O God, please let all strangers be afraid and fade away from their hiding places in my dreams in the name of Jesus.

Everlasting Father, please always make the entire operation of the enemy in my dreams to be a total failure in the name of Jesus.

O God, please let any satanic leg that entered my dreams be made to walk out permanently in the name of Jesus.

Everlasting Father, please let any evil foundation of my parents operating in my dreams, be changed to that of the Lord Jesus Christ in Jesus' name.

O God, please let all those enforcing satanic attachments to my dreams be permanently chased away by Your power in the name of Jesus.

At the end of this prayer, please make the following declarations based on Psalm 24:

This earth is God's, and the fullness thereof; the world and all who dwell therein, including my dreams. For God founded it upon the seas and established it upon the floods. Lift up your heads, O ye gates of my dreams; and the holy King of Glory shall come in to sanctify and deliver my dreams afresh in the name of Jesus. Who is this King of glory? The Lord, strong and mighty, the

Lord, mighty in battle. Lift up your heads, O ye gates of my dreams; and be ye lifted up, you ancient doors of my dreams; and the holy King of glory shall come in to uproot the forces of darkness from my dreams in the name of Jesus.

You can repeat the declarations as often as you are led by the Holy Spirit.
Thank God for answered prayers.

Chapter 9

THE FRUIT OF THE WOMB

Always refer to the section on forgiveness and praises before doing the prayers.

When God created man and woman, he spoke into their lives and said, 'Be fruitful and multiply.' This fruitfulness also relates to the fruit of the womb. Many scriptures in the Bible also support the view that child procreation is the will of God for our lives. The timing can vary with individuals. The cause of delay can be attributed to many varied reasons. These include God's own timing (Abraham and Sarah), hereditary factors, the presence of a curse, foundational enemy attacks, witchcraft, occultism, evil covenants, husband's sperm counts, damaged womb, previous sexual sins, medical error, etc.

Fortunately, if God takes interest in the problem, the adverse situation can be reversed because he is merciful and very knowledgeable about every part of the human body that he created. This is one of the reasons why we always need to present our problems to him in prayers.

You will find these prayers very useful if you pray them rightly and in faith.

Leviticus 26:3, 9 read:
"If ye walk in my statutes, and keep my commandments and do them For I will have respect unto you, and make you fruitful, and multiply you, and establish my covenant with you."
Everlasting Father, please have mercy on me, and forgive my previous misdeeds. Establish Your covenant with me and multiply me in Jesus' name.

Genesis 20:17 reads:
"So Abraham prayed unto God: and God healed Abimelech, and his wife, and his maidservants, and they bare children."
Just as the Holy God of multiplicity and power commanded Abraham to pray for Abimelech and his family so that he can release his fruits of the womb to them, most blessed Spirit of the living God, please intercede for me, and loose me from this reproach, and release my baby to me in the name of Jesus.

Exodus 23:26 reads:
"There shall nothing cast their young, nor be barren, in thy land: the number of thy days I will fulfil."
Everlasting Creator, I stand on these words that have gone out of Your mouth and declare in faith that they shall not return back to You void in my conception but will accomplish their purposed in Jesus' name.

Numbers 23:19 reads:

"God is not a man, that he should lie; neither the son of man, that he should repent: hath he said, and shall he not do it? or hath he spoken and shall he not make it good?"

O Holy God whose words are yea and amen to Your glory, please perfect Your words of fruitfulness in my womb today in the name of Jesus.

Isaiah 59:2 reads:

"But your iniquities have separated between you and your God, and your sins have hid his face from you, that he will not hear".

Pray like this:

O Lord God, to whom all souls belong, please forgive my sins and that of my ancestors. I am ashamed of them. Let the precious blood of Jesus wash them clean, and let Your promises in Exodus 23:26 (NIV) which says (paraphrased), "None shall miscarry or be barren in your land" be fulfilled in my life in the name of Jesus.

Isaiah 8:18 reads:

"Behold, I and the children whom the LORD hath given me, are for signs and for wonders in Israel from the LORD of hosts, which dwelleth in mount Zion."

According to the word of God in Exodus 23:26, which spoke children into my life, I claim them now in the name of Jesus. My Father and my God, the Only one whose words are Yea and amen to His glory, let the children You promised me spiritually come out now physically, as signs and wonders to Your glory in Jesus' name. Your words shall never fall to the ground in my life because I reverence You and believe in You in Jesus' name.

Psalm 126:5–6 reads:
"They that sow in tears shall reap in joy. He that goeth forth and weepeth, bearing precious seed for sowing, shall doubtless come again with rejoicing,
bringing his sheaves with him."
Everlasting Father, the God who is able to do exceeding abundantly above all that we ask or think, I claim Your promise of sowing in tears and reaping in joy in Jesus' name. Please let me, who so far has sown in tears at conception, now reap in joy to Your glory in Jesus' name.

Psalm 1:3 reads:
"And he shall be like a tree planted by the rivers of water, that bringeth forth his fruit in his season; his leaf also shall not wither; and whatsoever he doeth shall prosper."
O God of signs and wonders, please call forth Your seed into my womb, as a seed that will serve You in this world in Jesus Name. Let me be like a tree that is planted by the rivers of water, that will bring forth my fruit like the Hebrew women in due season in Jesus' name.
O Holy God of mercy, the great Restorer, please let all the faces that rejoiced at my childlessness be at hand to rejoice with me and glorify You for my conception and delivery in Jesus' name.
O God, please let every arrow of demonic delay, backwardness, and stagnation being fired against my

conception hit the ground and fail permanently in the name of Jesus.

Psalm 24:7–8 (paraphrased):
"Lift up your heads, O ye gates of my womb, and be ye lift up, ye everlasting doors of my conception, and the King of glory shall come in to glorify Himself. Who is this King of glory? The LORD strong and Mighty, the Lord Mighty in battle."
Pray this as many times as you want and then continue thus:
Father Lord, who gave Sara Isaac and Hannah Samuel, please command the doors of my womb to open and receive Your heritage in Jesus' name.
You, this womb, hear the words of the living God; after the orders of God in the book of Exodus 23:26; Leviticus 36:33, 9; and Psalm 128:3, receive your children now in the name of Jesus.

Romans 8:11 reads:
"But if the Spirit of him that raised up Jesus from the dead dwell in you, he that raised up Christ from the dead shall also quicken your mortal bodies by his Spirit that dwelleth in you."
Most blessed holy Spirit of the living God, please let Your fire quicken my womb to bring forth children to the glory of God in Jesus' name.
Pray this seven (7) times and plead the blood of Jesus seven (7) times over your womb.

Hebrews 10:19a reads:

"Having therefore, brethren, boldness to enter into the holiest by the blood of Jesus."

Holy God of multiplicity and growth, please let the same blood that defeated Satan, the author of evil, and ushered Christ into the holiest of holies, flush out all impurities in my womb and my husband's system in the name of Jesus.

O Lord, through the blood of Jesus, please remove all foundational hindrances to my conception in the name of Jesus.

Psalm 128:3 reads:

"Thy wife shall be as a fruitful vine by the sides of thine house: thy children like olive plants round about thy table. Behold, that thus shall the man be blessed that feareth the LORD."

Everlasting Father, please lead me into the right fear of You and make me a fruitful vine in my house in the name of Jesus.

Please let my children be like olive plants round about my table in the name of Jesus.

Psalm 127:3–4 reads:

"Lo, children are an heritage of the LORD; and the fruit of the womb is his reward.

As arrows are in the hand of a mighty man; so are the children of the youth."

Father Lord, please let my womb receive Your heritage in the name of Jesus, and let Your glory appear in the tabernacle of my womb in the name of Jesus.

Thank You, God, for answered prayers in Jesus' name.

Pray these prayers as often as you can. Pray them also in the middle of the night. He is a merciful God and He loves to bless.

Chapter 10

THE BLOOD OF JESUS

Satan has tried to duplicate everything that God created, but he can never place a duplicate on the blood of Jesus. It is the master piece creation of the Holy God and the replica of his holiness. Is Satan holy? Is there anyone around his kingdom that is holy to produce a replica? Whose blood will he use then? The defeat of Satan by the blood of Jesus is total, global and final. God passed on that victory to his children and in Revelation 12:11 says: "And they overcame him by the blood of the Lamb, and by the word of their testimony". When you quote the Word and the relevant scripture that pertains to the blood in faith, and present the problem to God, you may not be far from an answered prayer.

The scripture in Exodus 12:13 spoken by God Himself says:
"And when I see the blood, I will pass over you."
This means that the blood can exempt the Christians from harm. It is a protective cover. The use of the blood of Jesus like the word of God, is a powerful weapon for

warfare against Satan. Pray the following prayers:

O holy covenant-keeping God, please let the blood of Jesus, create a permanent demarcation between me and my enemies in the name of Jesus.

Father God, please whenever I plead the blood of Jesus with faith; let its powers be released to create a protective covering for me, in the mighty name of Jesus.

O God, please let anything that will make me to call the blood of Jesus in vain be permanently uprooted from my life in the name of Jesus.

O God, please let every organ that is malfunctioning in my body be washed whole by the power in the blood of Jesus.

Holy God, please let every spiritual object or animal projected into my body be flushed out by the blood of Jesus that I drink in Jesus' name.

Repeat seven (7) times: In the name of Jesus, I drink the blood of Jesus (demonstrate as you do so).

O Holy God, please let the power in the blood of Jesus flush out all impurities from my blood including the spirit of dream forgetfulness in the mighty name of Jesus.

Colossians 1:14 reads:

"In whom we have redemption through His blood, even the forgiveness of sins."

O God, please let the blood of Jesus cancel and nullify every association with any marine cult or any other evil association in my life in Jesus' name.

I use the blood of Jesus to break all covenants and curses

operating in my life and family in the name of Jesus.
Let the blood be a covenant and a refuge for me and my
family in the name of Jesus.

Exodus 7:20 reads:
"And Moses and Aaron did so, as the LORD commanded;
and he lifted up the rod, and smote the waters that were
in the river, in the sight of Pharaoh, and in the sight of
his servants; and all the waters that were in the river were
turned to blood."
Everlasting God of yesterday, today, and tomorrow,
please turn the black waters of my enemies to blood in
the name of Jesus.

Matthew 26:27–28 reads:
"Drink ye all of it; For this is my blood of the new
testament, which is shed for many for the remission of
sins."
O Holy God of all righteousness, please let anything that
opens the doorway of sin in my life be flushed out by the
everlasting blood of Jesus that I plead and drink in Jesus'
name.

Psalm 16:4 reads:
"Their sorrows shall be multiplied that hasten after
another god: their drink offerings of blood will I not
offer".
Everlasting Father and my Redeemer, please let the
precious blood of Jesus that has paid the price for me
now challenge the powers of my enemies who are hunting

for my blood and raging against what Jesus stands for in my life in the name of Jesus.

O God, please let the blood of Jesus become a garment and a shelter for me and every member of my family in the name of Jesus.

Revelation 1:5 reads:
"Unto him that loved us, and washed us from our sins in his own blood."
O most merciful God, please let the blood of Jesus cleanse and preserve us in holiness all the days of our lives in the mighty name of Jesus.

Ephesians 2:13 reads:
"But now in Christ Jesus ye who sometime were far off are made nigh by the blood of Christ."
O God of peace and righteousness, please let the power in the blood of Jesus foster unity in our families and in the body of Christ, and flush out every spirit of disobedience in Jesus' name.

Acts 17:26 reads:
"And hath made of one blood all nations of men for to dwell on all the face of the earth."
O God of power, please let the power in the blood of Jesus soak in and cover every hearer of the word, and draw them to Christ in the name of Jesus.

Revelation 5:10 reads:

"And hast made us unto our God kings and priests: and we shall reign on the earth."

Eternal Father of the whole world, O Holy God, please let the blood of Jesus that exalted us as kings and priests also protect and preserve us, and make us willing and able always to do thy good pleasure in Jesus' name.

John 6:53–54 reads:

"Verily verily, I say unto you, Except ye eat the flesh of the Son of man and drink his blood, ye have no life in you. Whoso eateth my flesh and drinketh my blood hath eternal life; and I will raise him up at the last day."

Everlasting Redeemer, please help me to always eat Your flesh and drink Your blood and attain eternal life in Jesus' name.

Ephesians 1:7 reads:

"In whom we have redemption through his blood, the forgiveness of sins according to the riches of his grace."

Ever true and faithful God, please let the blood of Jesus, through the riches of Your grace never depart from me as I run this race to get to You, my precious Redeemer, in Jesus' name.

Jeremiah 5:22 reads:

"Fear ye not me? saith the LORD: will ye not tremble at my presence, which have placed the sand for the bound of the sea by a perpetual decree, that it cannot pass it: and though the waves thereof toss themselves, yet can they not prevail."

O Lord, please put an everlasting fear of You in me, in the name of Jesus. O Thou everlasting God, the same yesterday, today, and forever, please let Your mighty hand that placed a boundary between the land and sea command the everlasting boundary of the blood of Jesus between me and foundational enemies never to be broken in the name of Jesus.

Revelation 5:9b reads:

"For thou wast slain, and hast redeemed us to God by thy blood out of every kindred, and tongue, and people, and nation".

O Holy God, please let the bond formed by the blood of Jesus between me and every redeemed with Christ never be broken by any satanic power in the name of Jesus.

Thou great Repairer, please let all the elements of my salvation be soaked in and transformed by the blood of Jesus in Jesus' name.

Exodus 24:8 reads:

"And Moses took the blood, and sprinkled it on the people, and said, Behold the blood of the covenant, which the LORD hath made with you concerning all these words."

O Holy God, please let the blood of Jesus speak permanent failure into every sinful act in my life, in the name of Jesus.

O holy covenant-keeping God, please let any unrighteousness in my life be cleansed by the shed blood Jesus' in Jesus name. I plead the blood of Jesus as a covering on my prayers and possessions in the name of Jesus.

I plead the blood of Jesus as a covering on my prayers and possessions in the name of Jesus.
O Holy God, please let the blood of Jesus always create a refuge for me in my dreams, in the mighty name of Jesus.

Luke 22:20 reads:
"Likewise also the cup after supper, saying, This cup is the new testament in my blood, which is shed for you."
O God, please let the blood of Jesus minister a new life to me, in Jesus' name. Empower me to sustain and illuminate the new life that the blood guarantees for me in the name of Jesus.

Luke 22:44 reads:
"And being in an agony he prayed more earnestly: and his sweat was as it were great drops of blood falling down to the ground."
Our everlasting Redeemer, please let Your precious blood of power always intercede and energize my prayers in the name of Jesus.

Acts 18:6 reads:
"And when they opposed themselves, and blasphemed, he shook his raiment, and said unto them, your blood be upon your heads; I am clean: from henceforth I will go

unto the Gentiles."
O Holy God of truth and life, please let not my sins, hidden and open, bring the judgment of the blood of Jesus against me. Please let the spirit of repentance and remission of sins overshadow my life, in the name of Jesus.

Hebrews 9:14 reads:
"How much more shall the blood of Christ who through the eternal Spirit offered Himself without spot to God, purge your conscience from dead works to serve the living God?"
Let Your blood, O precious Redeemer, purge my conscience of all dead works, and energize me to serve God faithfully and obediently in Jesus' name.
O God, please let all the plans of the enemy to secretly initiate me fail, in Jesus' name.
O God of power and might, please when I plead the blood of Jesus, let it always drive away the enemy from my life in Jesus' name.

Hebrews 9:12 reads:
"But by his own blood he entered once into the holy place, having obtained eternal redemption for us."
Most blessed and Holy God, because Christ by his own blood entered the holy place as my High Priest, please enable me to grow and maintain a complete state of righteousness with You in Jesus' name.
O God, please let the enemies of my salvation who indirectly took a covenant of death against the blood of Jesus in my life now realize that the blood will never die

again, and that they have failed forever in Jesus' name.

O Lord, please sanctify me with the blood of Jesus, and purify me with the fire of the Holy Ghost in Jesus' name.

Psalm 16:4 reads:

"Their sorrows shall be multiplied that hasten after another god: their drink offerings of blood will I not offer, nor take up their names into my lips."

My Holy God and Redeemer, please do not let the enemy use my blood or the blood of my family for a sacrifice, in the name of Jesus.

Holy God, please let the blood of Jesus nullify all satanic relationships in my dreams, in the name of Jesus.

O God, please let the power in the blood of Jesus defend the truth in my life, and nullify any relationship that will lead me to hell fire, in the name of Jesus.

1 Peter 1:18a–19 reads:

"For as much as ye know that ye were not redeemed with compatible things, as silver and gold ... But with the precious blood of Christ, as of a lamb without blemish and without spot."

Pray and demonstrate:

I wash my head with the blood of Jesus.

I wash my mind with the blood of Jesus.

I drink the blood of Jesus (seven (7) times).

I plead the blood of Jesus (three (3) times).

I move in the blood of Jesus (three (3) times).

Blood of Jesus, please fight for me (three (3) times)

Thank You, Lord, in Jesus' name.

Chapter 11

THE YOUTH AND THE YOUNG

Today's children are the leaders of tomorrow. They are living at a perilous time, the end time. This fact, fortunately or unfortunately, has to inform their behaviour as youths and future leaders.

Jesus lived in this world as a child, a youth, and a young man. All the hardship that is being experienced today had already been experienced by him. He emerged successful through obedience to God, His Father. He set an example for the youth and the young to obey. Youths should always pray that like Jesus, God will empower them to learn obedience through the sufferings they experience.

Are the youths of today prepared to follow Him in obedience to heaven? The choice is theirs to make. In order to follow Christ, it is necessary to develop His type of heart which is a heart of love, service, humility, and obedience.

They also need to ask God to turn their hearts away from

the enticements and the distractions of this world in Jesus' name. Jesus set an example of holiness, hard work, and obedience for the youths and the young to emulate.

John 14:6 reads:
"I am the way, the truth, and the life."
He is the only way to salvation and to God (John 10:9). He is the truth of what God stands for and what the Word says (John 17:17). He is the eternal life (John 1:4) that God has restored to us.

The young and the youth need very strong prayers, and most importantly, the help and guidance of the Holy Spirit in order to get through this age, and hold on fervently to Christ. They need the stepping stone of salvation and holiness in order to pass through this end time successfully. All these will help them to maintain a sound state of righteousness, spiritual growth, good health, academic progress, protection, etc., from God.

One common problem of youths whether in the secular or in the church, apart from distraction, centre on academic success and job prospects. The devil never wants anybody to pass their exams or get a good job. If prayers are not necessary, why do students still have to pray for God's intervention even after they have done a thorough revision of their academic work? Why do they experience sudden illness just before the set date for the examination? Why do they have attacks in dreams that sometimes lead to mistakes during exams which ordinarily they should not have made? Why are they subject to the spirit of temporary memory loss and confusion during the exams? Why the sudden loss of an important notebook a week or so before the exams? These are some of the problems that Satan can create in order to prevent people from making good grades in their exams. They need the guidance of the Holy Spirit at every stage of their lives.

Pray the following prayers based on the word. They can help you immensely. Firstly, refer to the section on forgiveness of sin, and praise and worship.

Psalm 128:1–2 reads:
"Blessed is everyone that feareth the LORD; that walketh in his ways. For thou shalt eat the labour of thine hands".
O most merciful God, the everlasting Rewarder of mankind, You have seen my consistency in Your work and in my studies. Please may I receive adequate reward for my efforts in Jesus' name.

Jesus said to the church at Ephesus in Revelation 2:2, "I know thy works, and thy labour and thy patience".
O Thou great and righteous God, please do not let me, Your child labour in vain in my academic work in the name of Jesus..
Please Holy God, let all the spiritual and human enemies who are hindering my spiritual and academic progress be permanently defeated in the name of Jesus.
Please empower me to persist diligently in my studies

despite the attempt of the enemies to bring interruptions on my way in the name of Jesus.

I bind from my studies the spirit of wandering thoughts and cast it away in the name of Jesus.

Matthew 11:28 reads:

"Come unto me, all ye that labour and are heavy laden, and I will give you rest."

O Holy God, the author of peace; please let Your peace and success that passes all understanding be bestowed on my studies in Jesus' name.

Psalm 34:11 reads:

"Come ye children, hearken unto me: I will teach you the fear of the LORD."

Proverbs 9:10 reads: "The fear of the LORD is the beginning of wisdom".

Holy God, I come to You as Your child who is growing in You. Please teach me Your fear that will usher in wisdom into my life in the name of Jesus.

Isaiah 40:30 reads:

"Even the youths shall faint and be weary, and the young men shall utterly fall: but they that wait upon the LORD shall renew their strength".

O God, my Redeemer, please give me the power to mount up with the wings of success in my exams. Let me study and never be tired in Jesus' name.

Isaiah 30:1 reads:

"Woe to the rebellious children, saith the LORD, that take counsel, but not of me; and that cover with a covering, but not of my spirit, that they might add sin to sin."

O God that watches over those that love Him, please give me the power to reject every spirit that is not of You, such as bad friends, sin of immorality, laziness, not studying the word of God regularly, devising evil in my heart, disobedience, etc. Envelope me with Your salvation and righteousness in Jesus' name.

Psalm 132:12 reads:

"If thy children will keep my covenant and my testimony that I shall teach them, their children shall also sit upon thy throne forevermore."

O thou holy covenant-keeping God, please give me the enabling grace to obey all Your words and to teach my children to do so, so that they will be heirs of thy kingdom in Jesus' name.

1 John 3:7–8a reads:

"Little children, let no man deceive you: he that doeth righteousness is righteous, even as he is righteous. He that comitteth sin is of the devil, for the devil sinneth from the beginning".

O Holy God of righteousness, please guide my steps far away from the paths of spiritual and human deceivers of my soul. Let not my efforts to live a holy life be suddenly terminated by any error on my path, in the name of Jesus.

Ezekiel 18:20 reads:

"The son shall not bear the iniquity of the father, neither shall the father bear the iniquity of the son: the righteousness of the righteous shall be upon him, and the wickedness of the wicked shall be upon him."

Thou holy and great Judge of mankind, please direct my steps away from the mistakes of my generations past. Enable me to emulate their successes and to learn a lesson from their mistakes, in the name of Jesus.

Matthew 19:14 reads:
"But Jesus said, Suffer little children, and forbid them not, to come unto me: for of such is the kingdom of heaven."

Father Lord, as I come to You in spirit, soul, and body, please lay Your hands of power, protection, and success upon me in the name of Jesus.

1 John 4:4 reads
"Ye are of God, little children, and have overcome them because greater is he that is in you than he that is in the world."

O Thou God, the strength of all children, please give me the grace to live a holy life, so that as the Holy Spirit indwells me, I can with faith overcome the works of darkness in the name of Jesus.

Psalm 127:3 reads:
"Lo children are an heritage of the LORD: and the fruit of the womb is His reward."

O God, my Righteousness, since I will inherit the

kingdom, please give me the grace to obey You, so that I can live holy, and fulfil all the laws of the kingdom in Jesus' name.

Psalm 127:4 reads:
"As arrows are in the hand of a mighty man: so are the children of the youth."
Holy Lord, please prepare me and shoot me out as Your arrow to carry the gospel to all parts of the universe in Jesus' name.

Daniel 5:12 reads:
"For as much as an excellent spirit, and knowledge, and understanding … were found in the same Daniel".
O Holy God of knowledge and truth, please endow me with the spirit of excellence, so that I shall always excel, not only in Your work and my relationship with other people, but also in my studies, in the name of Jesus.

1 John 5:21 reads:
"Little children, keep yourselves from idols."
O Holy God, my Guide and protector, please guide my eyes and steps away from bad literatures, films and movies, dangerous internet programmes, etc., that pollute and create idols in the hearts of people in Jesus' name. Guide me also on the path of truth, in Jesus' name.

Colossians 3:5–6 reads:
"Mortify therefore your members which are upon the earth; fornication, uncleanness, inordinate affection,

evil concupiscence, and covetousness, which is idolatry: for which things' sake the wrath of God cometh on the children of disobedience."

Our precious Redeemer, please give me the enablement to avoid all these sins listed in Colossians 3:5–6, which can bring down Your wrath upon me, in Jesus' name.

Matthew 13:38 reads:

"The field is the world; the good seed are the children of the kingdom; but the tares are the children of the wicked one."

My Maker and my Redeemer, please give me the grace to grow up as a good seed that loves, mends, and brings comfort to the soul, and not like the tares that kill, steal, destroy, and bring affliction to the soul in Jesus' name.

Matthew 5:9 reads:

"Blessed are the peacemakers: for they shall be called the children of God."

O Holy God, please teach me never to initiate trouble or fail to make peace with everybody in the mighty name of Jesus.

Daniel 1:4 reads:

"Children in whom was no blemish, but well favoured, and skilful in all wisdom, and cunning in knowledge and understanding science."

O God, please may I be numbered among the best in wisdom, knowledge, truth, and obedience to Your word in the name of Jesus.

Proverbs 4:1 reads:

"Hear, ye children, the instruction of a father and attend to know understanding."

Father, Lord, please give me the spirit of parental obedience and empower me not to undermine any advice of my parents that will lead me to wisdom, in Jesus' name.

Psalm 103:17 reads:

"But the mercy of the LORD is from everlasting to everlasting upon them that fear him, and his righteousness unto children's children."

O God, our Shepherd, please put the fear of You in my family, and let Your mercy and righteousness be an everlasting heritage in our lives in the name of Jesus.

Ecclesiastes 11:9 reads:

"Rejoice, O young man in thy youth; and let thy heart cheer thee in the days of thy youth, and walk in the ways of thine heart, and in the sight of thine eyes: but know thou, that for all these things God will bring thee into judgment."

Eternal Judge of the whole world, please give me the enabling grace to always look away from the sinful desires of the flesh that lead to condemnation and hell in Jesus' name.

2 Timothy 2:22 reads:

"Flee also youthful lusts; but follow righteousness, faith, charity, peace with them that call on the Lord out of a pure heart."

O Holy God, the Habitation of peace, please cleanse my heart, and make me walk in faith, charity, peace, and righteousness; for youthful lust is a snare in Jesus' name. "And a man's enemy shall be those of his household" (Matthew 10:36).

O Holy God, my Defender and Shield, please let any enemy in my household and my environment who has promised themselves that I shall not achieve my destiny fail permanently and witness my success in the mighty name of Jesus.

O God, please let any occult idolater from my background or houshold, working very hard to draw me away from the path of Christ be dislodged from their evil scheme in the name of Jesus.

John 9:4 reads:

"I must work the works of him that sent me, while it is day: the night cometh, when no man can work."

My Father and my God, please enable me to avoid procrastination, both in my work for You and in my academic work, so that I do not fail You in Jesus' name.

Proverbs 24:9 reads:

"The thought of foolishness is sin: and the scorner is an abomination to men."

Everlasting Father, please let the blood of Jesus and the fire of the Holy Ghost always cleanse and purify my thoughts, so that I do not fall into the sin of nursing foolish thoughts and scorn in my mind in the name of Jesus.

Psalm 32:8 reads:
"I will instruct thee and teach thee in the way which thou shalt go: I will guide thee with mine eye."
O God, my Shield and Guide, please enrol me in the spiritual training of the Holy Spirit, so that I can be safely led on the path of truth and not perish in the name of Jesus.

1 Thessalonians 5:17 reads:
"Pray without ceasing."
O Holy God, my Strength, please grant me the grace to live a prayerful life that is based, not only on my needs, but also on the need of others, in the name of Jesus.
Thank You, Holy God, for answered prayers, in Jesus' name.

Chapter 12

THE RIGHT MARRIAGE PARTNER

The main purpose of marriage is to provide a companion and a helpmate for the man. Those searching for life partners are perceived as being at crossroads by virtue of the fact that the entire process demands patience, extreme carefulness and seriousness, and continuous prayers to God if they are to locate their rightful partners. Any mistake they make will adversely affect the course of their lives. While on this process, Satan can project his own candidates in order to lead them away from their destinies. This unfortunate fact can be averted by being totally reliant on God and waiting patiently for Him to perfect the choice for you.

There are many instances in the Bible where God warned the Israelites against getting married to strangers. There are also many instances where such marriages caused a lot of havoc in the lives of the individuals concerned. A wrong choice can ignorantly block one's chances of making heaven. Since the scripture says that they are one flesh some misinterpret this to mean that even the scripture has to be modified for the interest of peace. Men like Samson, and Ahab, completely missed their destinies because of marrying the wrong people. God warned Solomon in 1 Kings 11:2 saying:

"Ye shall not go in to them, neither shall they come in unto you: for surely they will turn away your heart after their gods". This was exactly what happened. A man who pleased and exceled in the knowledge and wisdom of God was misled by strange women. We thank God for the spirit of repentance He bestowed on mankind.

2 Corinthians 6:14–17 warns:

"Be ye not unequally yoked together with unbelievers: for what fellowship has righteousness with unrighteousness? And what communion hath light with darkness? And what concord hath Christ with Belial? Or what part hath he that believeth with an infidel? And what agreement hath the temple of God with idols? … As God hath said; … wherefore come out from among them and be ye separate, saith the Lord, and touch not the unclean thing: and I will receive you."

There is no doubt; then, that this is a matter for a careful consideration before any decision is made or carried out.

Prayers should centre around the following factors:
- The need to be married to the right person
- Unforeseen hindrances
- The need to obey God
- Patience

- You have to follow your mind, not your eyes or flesh in this exercise

Hebrews 13:4 reads:
"Marriage is honourable in all, and the bed undefiled: but whoremongers and adulterers God will judge."
O Holy God, my Father, I have neither any knowledge nor light of my own, for all belong to You. Please guide me away from those who pretend to be what they are not, so that my married life will not be a failure in the name of Jesus.

Genesis 2:24 reads:
"Therefore shall a man leave his father and his mother, and shall cleave unto his wife: and they shall be one flesh."
O Holy God, the greatest Matchmaker, thank You for authorizing and blessing the act of marriage. Please bless me with the right marriage partner in Jesus' name.
Do not let me to go unmarried and be tempted to live out of Your word in Jesus' name.

Proverbs 18:22 reads:
"Whoso findeth a wife findeth a good thing, and obtaineth favour of the LORD."
Holy Father of all mercies, please give me the empowerment to search patiently and diligently for the right partner while following Your directives in the name of Jesus.

Proverbs 16:9 reads:

"A man's heart deviseth his way: but the LORD directeth his steps."

By Your everlasting mercy, O God, please direct my steps towards my destined marriage partner and against the will and desires of my enemies in the name of Jesus.

Nehemiah 13:27 reads:

"Shall we then hearken unto you to do all this great evil, to transgress against our God in marrying strange wives?"

O Holy God of truth, please do not let me be a victim of strange women in Jesus' name.

Let Your will be perfected in my choice of a life partner; one who is God-fearing and obedient to You in the name of Jesus.

Proverbs 21:1 reads:

"The king's heart is in the hand of the LORD, as the rivers of water: he turneth it wither so ever he will."

Please Holy God, condition my mind to understand what You are really trying to tell me about a life partner. Please speak to me in the language that I can understand in the name of Jesus.

Let any sin in my life that will make me search for Your voice unsuccessfully be made to disappear from my life in the name of Jesus.

Hosea 4:6 reads:

"My people are destroyed for lack of knowledge".

O God, the foundation of wisdom, please lead me to acquire all the relevant information I need in order to be able to make a wise decision about the right life partner in the name of Jesus.

Romans 12:10 reads:

"Be kindly affectioned one to another with brotherly love; in honour preferring one another."

My Father and my God, please help me to do away with any spirit of pride and lack of tolerance which are capable of working against my choice of a partner in the name of Jesus. Please help me to replace selfishness with love and understanding in the name of Jesus.

Foundational Hindrances

Ezekiel 18:20 reads:

"The son shall not bear the iniquity of the father, neither shall the father bear the iniquity of the son: the righteousness of the righteous shall be upon him".

My Father and my God, please do not let any carryover from my foundation adversely affect my choice of a marriage partner in the name of Jesus.

2 Corinthians 5:17 reads:

"Therefore if any man be in Christ, he is a new creature: old things are passed away; behold, all things are become new."

Everlasting Father, please let any demonic family pattern

of marriage dating from my ancestors, waiting to play itself out in my life, be cancelled by the power in the blood of Jesus in the name of Jesus.

Pray this prayer over the following evil family patterns, and personalize them. You can address them as the demonic pattern of:

Idolatry

Polygamy

Broken marriages

Poverty

Sexual immorality

Same sex children

Family curse

Evil covenants

Psalm 37:12 reads:

"The wicked plotteth against the just, and gnasheth upon him with his teeth."

Father Lord, please let any plan of the wicked aimed at diverting my rightful partner away from me spiritually or physically cease by Your power in the name of Jesus.

Matthew 10:36 reads:

"And a man's foes shall be they of his own household."

Everlasting Redeemer, please do not let me inherit enemies from the family in the name of Jesus. Give me the wisdom and love that I will need to deal with selfish and difficult in-laws; and let any satanic influence from the family militating against my search for the right partner fail permanently in Jesus' name.

The Right Choice

Jeremiah 29:11 reads:

"For I know the thoughts that I think toward you, saith the LORD, thoughts of peace and not of evil, to give you an expected end."

O God, the creator of knowledge, Your choice will always be better than mine. Please reveal to me the qualities of a life partner that will complement mine, so that my prayer will be more focused on what is right in the name of Jesus.

Proverbs 3:13 reads:

"Happy is the man that findeth wisdom, and the man that getteth understanding."

O God, my Guide, and my Strength, I pray for love of You God, wisdom, understanding, humility, patience, hard work and most importantly the knowledge of Your word as key qualities that I desire in a partner.

I stand on Your word in Luke 11:37 which states that "For with God nothing shall be impossible." Please grant my request in Jesus' name.

3 John 1:2 reads:

"Beloved, I wish above all things that thou mayest prosper and be in health, even as thy soul prospereth."

Merciful God of power and compassion, genuine prosperity comes from You. Please give me a partner that has the capability for unlimited spiritual and physical growth; and one that can endure temptation while exercising faith in Christ Jesus in Jesus' name.

Let the poverty that I experienced in my family, O God, not locate me in my marriage in the name of Jesus.

Deuteronomy 6:5 reads:
"And thou shalt love the LORD thy God with all thine heart, and with all thy soul, and with all thy might."
Holy God of love, please lead me to someone who, first and foremost, loves You with all his heart, soul, and might before anyone else in Jesus' name. Make us to be united in love for You and for our brethren in Jesus' name.

1 Peter 5:6 reads:
"Humble yourselves therefore under the mighty hand of God, that he may exalt you in due time."
My Father and my God, please give me a marriage partner, who will appreciate the overwhelming importance of humility in the life of a Christian, and live to be the same in the name of Jesus.

1 John 2:16 reads:
"For all that is in the world, the lust of the flesh, and the lust of the eyes, and the pride of life, is not of the Father, but is of the world. And the world passeth away, and the lust thereof: but he that doeth the will of God abideth for ever."
O God of truth and righteousness, please enable me to base my decision wisely on the word and not on lust and fleshly desires in the name of Jesus. Please do not let me lead my marriage partner into the sin of lust of the flesh before marriage in the name of Jesus.

Deuteronomy 7:14 reads:

"Thou shalt be blessed above all people. There shall not be male or female barren among you or among your cattle."

Bless my womb, O God, and let Your word in Deuteronomy 7:14 be operative in my life in order to glorify You in the name of Jesus.

Psalm 127:3 reads:

"Lo children are an heritage of the LORD: and the fruit of the womb is his reward."

O God of multiplicity, please do not allow me to become a victim of delayed conception; let Your heritage locate my womb immediately after marriage in Jesus' name.

John 5:17 reads:

"But Jesus answered them, My Father worketh hitherto, and I work."

O Lord of hosts, please give me a life partner who is obedient to the word, hardworking, and responsible in the name of Jesus.

Chapter 13

FAMILY PROBLEMS

The Word of God in Proverbs 19:14 states that a prudent wife is from the Lord. The word 'prudent' means carefulness and good judgement. What this means is that there is a need in the life of every married woman to make sure, by carefully adhering to the word of God, that a good and healthy relationship always exists, not only between her and her husband, but also between her and those she deals with; that she is careful in all that she does.

Some of the reasons why friction and disagreement tend to arise in some relationships can be attributed to the following factors: Unduly delayed pregnancy, financial constraints, evil foundation, lack of understanding and submission to each other, pride, infidelity, irresponsibility, disobedient children, etc. Prayers will be centred on these areas.

Delayed Pregnancy
Psalm 128:3 reads:
"Thy wife shall be as a fruitful vine by the sides of thine

house: thy children like olive plants round about thy table."

O most gracious and merciful God, please forgive my sins. Let the precious blood of Jesus flush out any sin that will disqualify me from the blessing of the womb. Make me a fruitful vine in my house in the name of Jesus.

Thou holy covenant-keeping God, please bless this marriage with your heritage in the name of Jesus. Any plan of the enemy to introduce any satanic delay in conception, please avert it in Jesus' name.

1 Timothy 2:15 reads:

"Notwithstanding, she shall be saved in child bearing, if they continue in faith and charity and holiness, with sobriety."

Father of all mercies; please guide us on the path of holiness, faith, love, and sobriety in the name of Jesus, so that at childbirth, we shall deliver like the Hebrew women in the name of Jesus (see the section on the fruit of the womb for more prayers).

Financial Constraint

Psalm 115:14 reads:

"The LORD shall increase you more and more, you and your children."

Everlasting God of multiplicity, please make us to experience the fullness of Your increase in this family in the name of Jesus.

Proverbs 3:9–10 says:

"Honour the LORD with thy substance, and with the first fruits of all thine increase:

So shall thy barns be filled with plenty, and thy presses shall burst out with new wine."

Father Lord, please let anything that will make us not to fulfil our financial obligations in the church and as a result, give rise to poverty, never get near to us in the name of Jesus.

Philippians 4:19 reads:

"But my God shall supply all your need according to his riches in glory by Christ Jesus."

Jehovah Jireh, the God of provision, please let Your provision for my family meet all our needs in the name of Jesus. Let us also have enough for the work of the Ministry and for charity in Jesus' name.

1 Timothy 5:18b reads:

"The labourer is worthy of his reward."

O most gracious Redeemer, please do not let us have to labour tirelessly without any financial benefits to show for it in Jesus' name.

Deuteronomy 28:4 reads:

"Blessed shall be the fruit of thy body, and the fruit of thy ground, and the fruit of thy cattle, the increase of thy kine, and the flocks of thy sheep."

O blessed God of all goodness, please lead us away from any sin that will make us not to reproduce, and as a result, deprive us, as a family, of Your blessings in the name of Jesus.

Matthew 6:24 reads:

"No man can serve two masters: for either he will hate the one, and love the other; or else he will hold to the one, and despise the other. Ye cannot serve God and mammon."

Everlasting Father of all truth, please do not let the divisive spirit of mammon control our finances. Please give us a healthy understanding of money, which is the root of all evil, according to Your word in the name of Jesus. May it not cause any frictions between us in the name of Jesus.

For more prayers on this section, please refer to the section on prosperity.

Evil Foundation

Galatians 3:13–14 reads:

"Christ hath redeemed us from the curse of the law, being made a curse for us: for it is written, Cursed is every one that hangeth on a tree. That the blessings of Abraham might come on the Gentiles through Jesus Christ, that we might receive the promise of the Spirit through faith."

O Holy God of might and power, please let any ancestral curse that is operating against the success of this marriage be broken in the name of Jesus.

We loose ourselves from every ancestral curse issued against this marriage by any enemy whether human or spiritual in the name of Jesus.

1 Kings 16:32 reads:
"And he reared up an altar for Baal in the house of Baal, which he had built in Samaria. And Ahab made a grove; and Ahab did more to provoke the LORD God of Israel to anger than all the Kings of Israel that were before him."
O Holy God, our Deliverer, please deliver us from any destructive influence of one married partner against the other, which could eventually lead the innocent one to hell fire. Please give us the wisdom to reject with love anything that contradicts Your word in the name of Jesus.

Genesis 12:1–2 reads:
"Now the LORD had said unto Abram, Get thee out of thy country, and from thy kindred, and from thy father's house, unto a land that I will show thee."
Father Lord, who foresees the end from the beginning, please protect this family from relatives and in-laws whose main interest centre on initiating the younger generation into ancestral cults, witchcraft, etc., in the name of Jesus.

Ecclesiastes 10:8 reads:
"He that diggeth a pit, shall fall into it; and whoso breaketh the hedge a serpent shall bite him."
O Holy God of all truth, please do not let us walk into any evil foundational pattern of the family, either consciously or in ignorance in the name of Jesus. O God,

please let all evil foundational strongholds that have attached themselves to this marriage be uprooted in the name of Jesus.

Ezekiel 18:20 reads:
"The soul that sinneth, it shall die. The son shall not bear the iniquity of the father, neither shall the father bear the iniquity of the son: the righteousness of the righteous shall be upon him and the wickedness of the wicked shall be upon him."
Please Holy Lord, based on this scripture, do not allow this family to inherit any evil ancestral load which she is not responsible for in the name Jesus.

Infidelity
Psalm 18:44–45 reads:
"As soon as they hear of me, they shall obey me; the strangers shall submit themselves unto me. The strangers shall fade away and be afraid out of their closed places."
O God of all righteousness, please preserve my marriage from the invasion of strangers whose purpose is to steal, to kill, and to destroy. Put a wall of fire around us, so that they do not come in at all in the name of Jesus.

1 Kings 11:1–3 lets us know that:
King Solomon in spite of his goodness and fear of God, was led astray by many strange women, concerning which the LORD said unto the children of Israel, "Ye shall not go in to them, neither shall they come in unto you". He was able to recognise his mistakes and write

against them.

Everlasting Father of all truth, please give to us the grace to be able to always keep away from all marriage seducers, both human and spiritual, in the name of Jesus. Empower us to remain faithful to Your pronouncements and to our marriage vow in the name of Jesus.

1 Corinthians 6:16–18 reads:

"What? Know ye not that he which is joined to an harlot is one body? For two, saith he, shall be one flesh. ... Every sin that a man doeth is without the body; but he that commiteth fornication sinneth against his own body."

O Thou Holy God, the Judge of all flesh, please do not let us fall into any sin of flesh in the name of Jesus.

1 Corinthians 3:16–17 reads:

"Know ye not that ye are the temple of God, that the Spirit of God dwelleth in you? If any man defile the temple of God, him shall GOD destroy; for the Temple of God is holy, which temple ye are."

My holy Father and my God, please let the blood of Jesus and the fire of the Holy Ghost dissociate my family and I from the satanic spirit of sexual aberration, currently prevalent in the world today; and give to us the enabling power to avoid bringing destruction to our bodies in the name of Jesus.

Pride

Proverbs 13:10 reads:

"Only by pride cometh contention, but with the well

advised is wisdom."
Father Lord, please give us the enablement to completely
give up pride in our lives and to humble ourselves and
learn of You in the name of Jesus.

1 John 2:16–17 reads:
"For all that is in the world, the lust of the flesh, and the
lust of the eyes, and the pride of life, is not of the Father,
but is of the world. And the world passeth away, and the
lust thereof: but he that doeth the will of God abideth
forever."
Eternal Father of life, may all the good things from You
never perish in our lives. Please give us the grace to get
rid of all that is of the flesh and to focus on Your word
alone in the name of Jesus.

2 Samuel 6:20–23b reads:
"And Michal the daughter of Saul came out to meet David
and said, How glorious was the King of Israel today, who
uncovered himself today in the eyes of the handmaids
of his servants as one of the vain fellows shamelessly
uncovereth himself. And David said unto Michal, It was
before the LORD which chose me before thy father and
before all his house, … Therefore Michal the daughter of
Saul, had no child unto the day of her death." This was as
a result of pride.
Eternal Judge of all flesh, please teach me to be humble
and careful of the advice I give to my husband or wife in
the name of Jesus.

Proverbs 22:4 reads:

"By humility and the fear of the LORD are riches, and honour, and life."

Holy Father, God, You are our example of humility in this world. Please let my family be established on the foundation of humility and a genuine fear of You in the mighty name of Jesus.

1 Corinthians 7:34b–35 reads:

"But she that is married careth for the things of the world, how she may please her husband. And this I speak for your own profit; not that I may cast a snare upon you, but for that which is comely, and that ye may attend upon the LORD without distraction."

Everlasting Father, please have mercy and forgive me for having neglected Your affairs selfishly while concentrating on my husband's. Please enlighten me in the knowledge of my role for You in Jesus' name.

Submission

Rom 5:3–4 reads:

"And not only so, but we glory in tribulations also, knowing that tribulations worketh patience; and patience experience, and experience, hope."

Holy Spirit, please guide us through Your spiritual training, so that we can be able to endure without complaint all the challenges that will arise in this marriage in the name of Jesus.

Ephesians 5:21–22, 25a reads:

"Submitting yourselves one to another in the fear of God. Wives, submit yourselves unto your own husbands, as unto the Lord. ... Husbands, love your wives, even as Christ also loved the church".

Everlasting Father of love, please impart in us the right spirit that will enable us to be and remain willingly submissive one to another in the love of Godin the name of Jesus.

Proverbs 31:10–12 reads:

"Who can find a virtuous woman? For her price is far above rubies. The heart of her husband doth safely trust in her, so that he shall have no need of spoil. She will do him good and not evil all the days of her life."

Father Lord, please endow me with the spirit of humility, wisdom, and love of the virtuous woman, so that my husband can repose confidence in mean the name of Jesus.

Disobedient Children

2 Timothy 3:1–2 reads:

"This know also, that in the last days perilous times shall come. For men shall be lovers of their own selves, covetous, boasters, proud, blasphemers, disobedient to parents, unthankful, unholy."

Parents who are too busy to impart the true knowledge and the character of Christ have children who grow up to manifest the characteristics of 2 Timothy 3:1–2.

Holy God, please give us the wisdom and understanding to rear God-fearing and obedient children in the name

of Jesus.

Proverbs 10:1 reads:
"A wise son makes a glad father: but a foolish son is the heaviness of his mother."
Father God of truth, please give to us children who are willing to obey You and will not be led astray by evil company in the name of Jesus.

James 1:22
"But be ye doers of the word, and not hearers only, deceiving your own selves."
Holy God of truth, please give us the grace to be true reflection of what the word is teaching us, so that our children will have a better and an easier understanding of the word in Jesus' name.

Proverbs 3:1–2
"My son, forget not my law; but let thine heart keep my commandments, for length of days, and long life, and peace, shall they add to thee."
Everlasting Creator of the whole world, who can extend our days and multiply our years, please keep us alive to train our children, so that they do not go astray in Jesus' name.

Psalm 127:4–5
"As arrows are in the hand of a mighty man; so are the children of the youth. Happy is the man that hath his quiver full of them: they shall not be ashamed, but shall

speak with the enemies in the gate."

Our Holy Father and our Provider, please let anything about our children that will bring us shame and defeat before our enemies be cancelled for ever in the name of Jesus.

Refer to the chapter on the young and the youth.

Chapter 14

THE RECONCILIATION OF MARRIED COUPLES

The Steps in Reconciliation:
Repentance
Confession
Reconciliation
Restitution

Reconciliation is the ministry that Jesus came to this earth to fulfil between God and man. The theme of reconciliation runs through both the Old and the New Testament in the Bible. Every act of reconciliation should be based on the peace of Christ.

2 Corinthians 5:18 reads:
"And all things are of God, who hath reconciled us to himself by Jesus Christ, and hath given to us the ministry of reconciliation."
This scripture seriously questions the idea of separation or divorce in marriages. If your relationship with your spouse is based on the love and peace of God in Christ

Jesus, who has reconciled you to himself, the need to separate yourself from your spouse may not arise.

Prayers

In Matthew 5:32 Jesus says:

"But I say unto you, That whosoever shall put away his wife, saving for the cause of fornication, causeth her to commit adultery; and whosoever shall marry her that is divorced committeth adultery."

O God of Abraham, Isaac, and Jacob, please forgive us for disobeying this scripture on marriage. I repent on behalf of my spouse and say that we are truly sorry. Please let the blood of Jesus wash away our sins and reunite us together again in thy love in Jesus' name.

Hebrews 2:17 reads:

"Wherefore in all things it behoved him to be made like unto his brethren, that he might be a merciful and faithful high priest in things pertaining to God, to make reconciliation for the sins of the people."

Almighty God, as the Ministry of Reconciliation of Your beloved Son Jesus Christ has continued in heaven, where he makes intercession for us, please let mine continue in all my relationships with other people, even after You have reconciled me to my spouse, in Jesus' name.

Hebrews 7:25 reads:

"Wherefore he is able also to save them to the uttermost that come unto God by him, seeing he ever liveth to make intercession for them."

Ever loving and merciful Jesus, please intercede for me and my spouse, so that we can be reconciled again and be able to live according to Your will in the name of Jesus.

Daniel 9:24 reads:

"Seventy weeks are determined upon thy people and upon thy holy city, to finish the transgression, and to make an end of sins, and to make reconciliation for iniquity and to bring in everlasting righteousness".

Most merciful God of reconciliation, please give my spouse and I the grace to make an end of iniquity by reconciling and living a righteous life in Christ Jesus, our Lord.

Please give us another chance to start a new life in You, our Reconciler, in Jesus' name.

Romans 5:10 reads:

"For if, when we were enemies we were reconciled to God, by the death of his Son, much more, being reconciled, we shall be saved by his life."

Everlasting Father of peace, as we were reconciled to You while still in our sins, please give to us the enablement to put all past disagreements behind us and live together in peace in Jesus' name.

Matthew 5:23–24 reads:

"Therefore if thou bring thy gift to the altar, and there rememberest that thy brother hath ought against thee; leave there thy gift before the altar, and go thy way; first be reconciled to thy brother, and then come and offer thy gift."

Holy Father, God, Your will is that I should be reconciled to my spouse. When next I make contact or go to him, please let me receive a favourable response in the name of Jesus.

Proverbs 21:1 reads:

"The King's heart is in the hand of the LORD, as the rivers of water: he turneth it whithersoever he will."

Everlasting Father of glory, the heart of my spouse is in Your hands. Please turn it away from anger and unforgiveness to a desire for me again in the mighty name of Jesus.

Proverbs 21:16 reads:

"The man that wandereth out of the way of understanding shall remain in the congregation of the dead."

Father, God, please give to us a good understanding of Your word that will enable us to sort out our differences amicably in the name of Jesus.

1 Corinthians 15:33 reads:

"Be not deceived: evil communications corrupt good manners."

Everlasting Judge of all flesh, please let all the satanic advice given against this marriage be identified, disgraced, and disregarded in the mighty name of Jesus.

Ephesians 5:25 reads:

"Husbands love your wives, even as Christ also loved the church".

Holy Father God of love, please light up the fire of Your love in the heart of my spouse, so that he will feel right towards me in the name of Jesus.

Isaiah 63:9 reads:

"In all their affliction he was afflicted, and the angel of his presence saved them: in his love and in his pity he redeemed them; and he bare them, and carried them all the days of old."

Merciful Father, please delegate the angel of Your presence to heal the wounds of this marriage in the name of Jesus.

2 Corinthians 5:21 reads:

"For he hath made him to be sin for us, who knew no sin; that we might be made the righteousness of God in him,"

O Holy God, if Your beloved Son bore my sins on the Cross, and if Your word says that we should esteem others higher than we are, please help me to bear my spouse's sins and be fully reconciled to him in Jesus' name.

Ephesians 2:16 reads:

"And that he might reconcile both unto God in one body by the cross, having slain the enmity thereby."

O Holy God, the strength of my life, please give me the power to destroy the ill-feeling and estrangement between my spouse, and me in Jesus' name. Please draw us back to each other again in the name of Jesus.

Colossians 1:21 reads:
"And you, that were sometime alienated and enemies in your mind by wicked works, yet now hath he reconciled."
O God, the author of reconciliation, please let the spirit of reconciliation grow and reproduce in our lives in the name of Jesus.

Acts 7:60 reads:
"And he kneeled down, and cried with a loud voice, Lord, lay not this sin to their charge. And when he had said this, he fell asleep."
Everlasting Father of all righteousness, since the relevant issue is not of human judgement but of You, please give us the enabling grace to forgive in times of extreme persecution and afflictions in the name of Jesus.

Proverbs 16:18 reads:
"Pride goeth before destruction, and an haughty spirit before a fall."
O holy Lord, my Teacher, please teach me to value others better than myself all the days of my life, so that I can avoid the destructive pit of pride in the name of Jesus.

Acts 17:28 reads:
"For in him we live, and move, and have our being".
Father Lord, in You, my marriage will live, move, and have its being. Please use it to achieve Your purposes in

this world in the name of Jesus.

Chapter 15

THE CHURCH

Christ laid the foundation of the church with His blood when He won salvation for mankind. He deposited His powers there before He ascended into heaven. It is the solution ground where the power and love of God is exemplified. The scripture makes reference to the Church under different names: the body of Christ (Ephesians 4:12), the holy temple (Ephesians 2:21), the pillar and ground of truth (1 Timothy 3:15), a chosen generation (1 Peter 2:9), a royal priesthood (1 Peter 2:9), the righteousness of God (2 Corinthians 5:21), the household of faith (Galatians 6:9), etc.

The Church is supposed to manifest all the powers that God deposited there; powers of love, holiness and righteousness, miracles, signs, and wonders, soul winning, counselling, training, etc. He spoke power into the Church.

In Matthew 16:19, He says:
"And I will give unto thee the keys of the kingdom of

heaven: and whatsoever thou shalt bind on earth shall be bound in heaven: and whatsoever thou shalt loose on earth shall be loosed in heaven."

This scripture is very invaluable, especially in deliverance exercises, and believers are very grateful to God for it. It means that by using it rightly, God can control the current works of darkness as well as set bondages free in the name of Jesus.

Matthew 18:19–20 reads:

"Again I say unto you, That if two of you shall agree on earth as touching anything that they shall ask, it shall be done for them of my Father which is in heaven. For where two or three are gathered together in my name, there I am in the midst of them."

This is a very strong pronouncement that releases faith for prayers to be answered, even till today..

John 14:12–13 reads:

"Verily, verily, I say unto you, He that believeth on me, the works that I do shall he do also; and greater works than these shall he do; because I go unto my Father. And whatsoever ye shall ask in my name, that will I do, that the Father may be glorified in the Son."

This means that it is possible, at least, to repeat some of those miracles which Christ performed when he was in this world if all requirements are met. In Matthew 17:20, He says: "If you have faith as a grain of mustard seed, you shall say unto this mountain, Remove hence to yonder place, and it shall remove; and nothing will be impossible unto you." In Luke 10:19, Mark 17–16:19, etc., the scripture gives other areas of the power He vested in the Church before He ascended into Heaven.

We are required to pray always for the Church, so that these powers will continue to be realized, and that all shall be the benefactors of this power. The Word of God in Matthew 13:21b tells us that persecution arises because of the Word. 1 Thessalonians 1:6b also tells us that the word was received with much affliction and joy of the Holy Ghost.

1 Thessalonians 1:6b also tells us that the word was received with much affliction and joy of the Holy Ghost. The Church is currently under severe attack in some countries. Many Christians are persecuted and some are slaughtered in cold blood on a regular basis. (China, India Pakistan, Indonesia Iran, Egypt etc) Some of these countries with repressive laws against Christians restrict them the freedom to practice their religion. Many are languishing in prisons.

Pray:

O Holy God of our salvation, please give the church the grace to intercede, on a regular basis, for all the Christians who are currently being held or undergoing one form of persecution or the other for the sake of Christ.

Sabina Wurmbrand, who, in conjunction with her husband, a pastor, founded The Voice of the Martyrs, said, "Leprosy is a disease without pain. No remedy is found because the nerves do not work. Lepers lose their fingers and toes in accidents because they cannot feel any pain. When the Church does not feel pain with those that are part of them, the Church's nerves have also become dead. Then the Church loses part of its body. It loses the power to touch souls. The Church loses its credibility to the world. On the other hand, the suffering Church gives the whole church strength to fight for Christ."

This statement should touch the soul of every believer, and encourage them to intercede more for the Church and its suffering members.

Prayers

O God, our Strength and Redeemer, please do not allow any affliction from the enemy to affect the zeal and the determination of the Church and individuals who are currently under persecution in the name of Jesus. Father Lord, please give unto the body of Christ the grace to persevere in interceding for Christians under persecution for the word, in the name of Jesus.

Romans 8:17 reads:

"And if children, then heirs; heirs of God, and joint-heirs with Christ; if so be that we suffer with him, that we may be also glorified together."

The unchanging and everlasting Father, please make the body of Christ a willing part of the persecutions that Jesus endured for her, so that she can glorify Him in the name of Jesus.

O God, please do not allow any of the 'bones' of those under serious persecution to be broken in the name of Jesus.

Acts 5:18–19 reads:

"And laid their hands on the apostles, and put them in the common prison. But the angel of the LORD by night opened the prison doors, and brought them forth".

My Father and my God, please stretch forth Your hand of power and mercy towards all Christians currently being held in prisons because of the Word, and minister deliverance to them in the mighty name of Jesus.

Ephesians 3:10–11 reads:

"To the intent that now that the manifold wisdom of God might be made known by the church to the principalities and powers in the heavenly places. … According to the eternal purpose which he purposed in Christ Jesus our Lord".

Everlasting Father of all power, please continue to release into the body of Christ the enablement to give back to the whole world Your successes and achievements in the life of Christ our Lord; so that the kingdom of darkness will come to the realization that in the Church You are the same as in the apostolic days in the name of Jesus.

Ephesians 1:17–18 reads:

"That the God of our LORD Jesus Christ, the Father of glory, may give unto you the spirit of wisdom and revelation in the knowledge of him: the eyes of your understanding being enlightened; that ye may know what is the hope of his calling, and what the riches of the glory of his inheritance in the saints."

Eternal God of all wisdom and knowledge, please make

Your Church to excel in wisdom and understanding. Let all believers progress towards spiritual maturity, so that they will greatly appreciate the power of their salvation in Jesus' name.

1 Corinthians 1:12–13 reads:
"Now this I say, that every one of you saith, I am of Paul; and I of Apollos; and I of Cephas; and I of Christ. Is Christ divided? Was Paul crucified for you? or were ye baptized in the name of Paul?"
Almighty Jehovah, the foundation of our salvation in Christ Jesus, please let the understanding of the fact that Jesus Christ through the power of the Holy Spirit is the only ground for unity in the Church. Let this fact be in the heart of every believer in the name of Jesus. Let them know that it is not geographical boundary, colour, ethnicity, or sex education that makes for Christian unity.
Enable all members of the Church to develop a selfless attitude in their relationship with others in Jesus' name.
Let the feeling of superiority disappear from the body of Christ in Jesus' name.

1 Corinthians 11:26–27 reads:
"For as often as ye eat this bread, and drink this cup, ye do shew the Lord's death till he come. Wherefore whosoever shall eat this bread, and drink this cup of the Lord unworthily, shall be guilty of the body and blood of the Lord."
Thou Holy God our Creator, please forgive those who

neglect to offer the Lord's Supper which is to be given regularly and those who receive it unworthily, in the name of Jesus. Let all partakers not forget the fact that the celebration testifies to the victory on the Cross. Father Lord, as we celebrate this victory, please help us to receive forgiveness, healing, wholeness, and restoration in Jesus' name.

Revelations 2:4 reads:
"Nevertheless I have somewhat against thee, because thou hast left thy first love."
O Holy God, please help the body of Christ, to develop true love in our lives for God and for our brethren, so that we shall be totally devoted and committed to Your word in Jesus' name. Please let the spiritual vitality we had for You at first be rebirthed in us again in the name of Jesus.

Revelations 2:13–14 reads:
"I know thy works, and where thou dwellest, even where Satan's seat is; and thou holdest fast my name and hast not denied my faith. ... But I have a few things against thee, because thou hast there them that hold the doctrine of Balaam".
O Holy God of all faithfulness and righteousness, please let Your Church live in the faith that can move mountains, especially at this period of strong persecution in the name of Jesus. Please give the Church the enabling wisdom to deal with those within the fold, who hold anti-Christ doctrines that mislead Your children in Jesus' name.

Ephesians 5:27 reads:

"That he might present it to himself a glorious church, not having spot, or wrinkle, or any such thing; but that it should be holy and without blemish."

O Holy God of power and might, please give to the Church the enablement to get rid of its weaknesses and live a life of holiness and righteousness in Jesus' name.

Ephesians 4:11–12 reads:

"And he gave some, apostles; and some, prophets; and some evangelists; and some, pastors and teachers; for the perfecting of the saints, for the work of the ministry, for the edifying of the body of Christ".

Father of all mercies, please give the church leaders or shepherds of Your flock the grace to develop, encourage, and nurture the individual and co-operate ministries of those that they lead in Jesus' name.

Ephesians 4:3–5 reads:

"Endeavouring to keep the unity of the Spirit in the bond of peace. There is one body, and one Spirit, even as ye are called in one hope of your calling. One Lord, one faith, one baptism".

Father God, please empower the Church to maintain the unity of the spirit which was typical of the Church in the apostolic days, in the name of Jesus.

Ephesians 4:30 reads:

"And grieve not the holy Spirit of God, whereby ye are sealed unto the day of redemption."

O God, please let any satanic agent, human or spiritual, whom You have not planted in the body of Christ, and is currently masquerading as the Holy Spirit, be uprooted in the name of Jesus.

Ephesians 5:8–9 reads:
"For ye were sometimes darkness, but now are ye light in the Lord: walk as children of light: (For the fruit of the Spirit is in all goodness and righteousness and truth)".
Eternal Father of glory, please may the Church steadfastly follow the path of Christ and walk in love and holiness, manifesting the fruits of the Spirit. Let her be a light to the world in Jesus' name.

Ephesians 6:17–18 reads:
"And take the helmet of salvation, and the sword of the Spirit, which is the word of God; Praying always with all prayers and supplications in the Spirit, and watching thereunto with all perseverance and supplication for all saints."
Everlasting Father of all knowledge, please let the body of Christ have a clear perception of Your word and its operations in their lives. Let their prayers be empowered and directed by You, and give her the grace to endure all temptations in the name of Jesus.

Ephesians 3:17–19 reads:
"That Christ may dwell in your hearts by faith; that ye, being rooted and grounded in love, may be able to comprehend with all saints, what is the breadth and

length, and depth, and height; and to know the love of Christ, which passeth knowledge".

Father God, I pray that all believers will always experience Your love and fullness spiritually and physically, and live to manifest the same in the name of Jesus.

Acts 2:46–47 reads:

"And they, continuing daily with one accord in the temple, and breaking bread from house to house did eat their meat with gladness and singleness of heart, praising God, and having favour with all the people. And the Lord added to the church daily such as should be saved."

O God, the Father of peace and all increase, please let the spirit of peace, contentment, sharing, and favour abide among the brethren of God so that they can work in unity towards Your purpose in Jesus' name.

Let the hunger to render praise and worship to You always grow in them; and let them be able to attract increase in numbers by doing these in Jesus' name.

Acts 20:28–29 reads:

"Take heed therefore unto yourselves, and to all the flock, over the which the Holy Ghost hath made you overseers, to feed the Church of God, which he hath purchased with his own blood. For I know this, that after my departing, shall grievous wolves enter in among you not sparing the flock."

O Holy God, the Author of salvation, please let fear and reverence for You possess all Overseers and leaders in authority in Your Church, so that they can tend properly the flocks under their charges in Jesus' name.

O God, please let the Church be protected against the menace of false teachers in the name of Jesus.

Romans 12:6 reads:

"Having then gifts differing according to the grace that is given to us, whether prophecy, let us prophesy according to the proportion of faith."

Father Lord, please I pray for a special grace to enable all Christians to be faithful and fervent in their conduct with regards to their ministries and callings in the name of Jesus.

Romans 12:10 reads:

"Be kindly affectioned one to another with brotherly love; in honour preferring one another."

Holy Lord Jesus, Your death for me on the Cross has said it all. Please release the anointing of humility on the entire church, so that members will perceive themselves not better than others in the name of Jesus.

1 Timothy 3:15 reads:

"But if I tarry long, that thou mayest know how thou oughtest to behave thyself in the house of God, which is the church of the living God, the pillar and ground of truth."

O Holy God, please let the Church's primary function of honouring God and spreading the truth of Christ never be undermined or cease to be accorded the priority they deserve in Jesus' name.

1 Tim 4:16 reads:

"Take heed unto thyself, and unto the doctrine; continue in them: for in doing this thou shalt both save thyself, and them that hear thee."

Everlasting Father of glory, please may the entire body of Christ always be empowered to examine themselves carefully in order to make sure that they are a living example of Christ to all who are saved and yet to be saved in Jesus' name.

1 Timothy 3:2, 7–9 reads:

"A bishop then must be blameless, the husband of one wife, vigilant, sober, of good behaviour, given to hospitality, apt to teach; … Moreover he must have a good report of them which are without; lest he fall into reproach and the snare of the devil. Likewise must the deacons be grave".

Holy God, Thou Judge of the whole world, please let only spiritually matured Christians be appointed to the office of leadership in the Church.

O God, please bestow on the leaders occupying the posts of bishops, deacons, etc., the spirit of holiness, faithfulness, and exemplary service.

May they not be found wanting in their private and pastoral duties in the name of Jesus.

Colossians 1:18–19 reads:

"And he is the head of the body, the church: who is the beginning, the firstborn from the dead; that in all things he might have the pre-eminence. For it pleased the

Father that in him should all fullness dwell."
Father God, as the shepherds perceive Jesus as superior and pre-eminent, let their actions be a testimony of His greatness and accomplishments in Jesus' name.

Ephesians 4:1–3 reads:
"I therefore, the prisoner of the Lord, beseech you that ye walk worthy of the vocation wherewith you are called, with all lowliness and meekness, with longsuffering, forbearing one another in love, endeavouring to keep the unity of the Spirit in the bond of peace."
O God, please instil in all believers the need to live a life characterized by love, joy, peace, longsuffering, gentleness, goodness, faith, meekness, temperance, which are the fruits of the Spirit.
1 Corinthians 13:2–3 reads:
"And though I have the gift of prophecy, and understand all mysteries and all knowledge; and though I have all faith, so that I could remove mountains, and have not charity, I am nothing."
Most merciful God of Abraham, Isaac, and Jacob, please let the body of Christ become a great citadel of agape love in Jesus' name.

Revelation 2:2a, 4 reads:
"I know thy works, and thy labour, and thy patience, and how thou canst not bear them which are evil: and thou hast tried them which say they are apostles, and are not, and hast found them liars. ... Nevertheless, I have somewhat against thee, because thou hast left thy

first love."
O Holy God, the habitation of love, please do not allow the Church to backslide in any of its duties towards You. Let the vitality of devotion they started with be restored in the mighty name of Jesus.

Revelation 2:8–10 reads:
"And unto the angel of the church in Smyrna write; … I know thy works, and tribulation, and poverty (but you are rich) … and ye shall have tribulation ten days: be thou faithful unto death, and I will give thee a crown of life."
Please holy Father, strengthen the body of Christ spiritually, so that it will learn to accept all the hardships and rough roads that it has to pass in the journey to the kingdom, in the name of Jesus.
Eternal Judge of mankind, please let the church come to a full realization that obeying half or three quarters of the word will not necessarily get one anywhere to heaven, but in obeying the whole lot.
Let the Church always experience revival, spiritual, and physical growth in Jesus' name.

The Salvation of the Mind
If you can win the battle of the mind, it is said, you can win any other battle.
If you can succeed in driving Satan and his satanic suggestions and advice away from your mind, you will not be far from the Kingdom. This is why these prayers require seriousness and regularity. Firstly, refer to prayers

on praises and forgiveness.

Luke 11:34 reads:
"But when thine eye is evil, thy body also is full of darkness."
It is the eye that darkens the thoughts of the mind. I plead and soak my eyes in the blood of Jesus in Jesus' name.
O Holy God, the Judge of the mind, please let any darkness in my eyes and mind be washed away by the living blood of Jesus which was shed for the destruction of evil in the name of Jesus.
Most merciful God, please let the spirit of righteousness overshadow my mind and thoughts in the name of Jesus.
I bind the spirit of fear and cast it out of my mind in the name of Jesus.

Matthew 18:9 reads:
"And if thine eye offend thee, pluck it out, and cast it from thee; it is better for thee to enter into life with one eye, rather than having two eyes to be cast into hellfire."
Please God, give me the empowerment to focus and keep under strict control my wondering thoughts in the name of Jesus. Do not allow the wondering of my eyes to introduce distractions into my mind that will lead me to hell fire in Jesus' name.
Please God, give me the power to exercise control over my mind, even in the dream, in the name of Jesus.
O Lord, please command discipline into my eyes and my mind in the mighty name of Jesus.
I draw strength from You, O Holy God, to focus my

mind always on You and Your word in the name of Jesus.

Isaiah 26:3 reads:

"You will keep him in perfect peace, whose mind is stayed on You, because he trusteth in You."

Please Holy God, give me the power to extricate my mind from sinful thoughts and to base them on You alone in Jesus' name. Please help me to fight and win the battle of the mind in Jesus' name. O God, please let Your strength be made perfect in the wanderings of my thoughts and mind in Jesus' name.

Romans 8:5–6 reads:

"For they that are after the flesh do mind the things of the flesh; but they that are after the Spirit the things of the Spirit. For to be carnally minded is death, but to be spiritually minded is life and peace."

O God, please teach me to focus my mind on the things of the Spirit. Let my mind receive the anointing for spiritual growth that leads to life and peace in Jesus' name.

Romans 12:2 reads:

"And be not conformed to this world: but be ye transformed by the renewing of your mind, that ye may prove what is that good, and acceptable, and perfect, will of God."

O God, my strength and shield, please impart to me the power to transform my thoughts into goodness, so that I can live and work according to Your will in the name

of Jesus.

Father, God, please take complete control of the movement of my mind and thoughts in the name of Jesus.

Proverbs 21:1 reads:

"The king's heart is in the hand of the LORD, as the rivers of water: he turneth it whithersoever he will."

My High Tower and my Salvation, please always turn my heart and thoughts towards Your ways and how to please You in the name of Jesus. Turn my heart away from anything that will go against Your will in the name of Jesus. Please anoint my mind to always and automatically reject every satanic lies and distractions programmed against it in the name of Jesus. Empower me, also, to completely detach my mind from the things of this world; to base them on spiritual and enduring things, in the name of Jesus.

1 Peter 1:13 reads:

"Wherefore gird up the loins of your mind, be sober, and hope to the end for the grace that is to be brought unto you at the revelation of Jesus Christ."

O Holy God, my Light, please give me the grace to be able to direct the thoughts of my mind towards relevant acts of endurance, perseverance, righteousness, and hard work in the face of temptations at this end time in the mighty name of Jesus. Please always possess my mind and direct my thoughts in the name of Jesus. Let Your word live and reproduce in my heart in the name

of Jesus.

Hebrews 8:10b reads:
"I will put my laws into their mind, and write them in their hearts: and I will be to them a God, and they shall be to me a people."
Everlasting Father, please let Your covenant relationship of grace in my heart and mind minister the knowledge of Your truth to me, so that my feelings will be purified in the name of Jesus. Let Your law in my mind and written in my heart become fire and consume anything that is not of God in my body and life in the name of Jesus.

Philippians 2:5 reads:
"Let this mind be in you, which was also in Christ Jesus"
O Holy God, my Creator, please impart on me a heart of humility and love, which is completely emptied of its rights, in the name of Jesus.
Please God, hide my mind in Your heart, and monitor my thoughts from there in Jesus' name. Do not allow me to break Your covenant with me in my heart in Jesus' name.

James 4:8 reads:
"And purify your hearts, ye double minded."
Everlasting God, please sanctify me; enable me to purge my heart of all sinful thoughts and let it be for You alone in Jesus' name.

Pray with Psalm 24:

"The earth is the LORD'S, and the fullness thereof; the world and they that dwell therein. For he hath founded it upon the seas, and established it upon the floods. Who shall ascend into the hill of the LORD? Or who shall stand in his holy place? He that hath clean hands, and a pure heart; who hath not lifted up his soul unto vanity, nor sworn deceitfully. ... Lift up your heads, O ye gates (my mind and heart); and be ye lift up, ye everlasting doors; and the King of glory shall come in (to sanctify and possess my thoughts)."

You can put any of the following as it pertains to you at the dotted lines Sickness and infirmity, poverty, delayed conception, dream attack, sinfulness, disappointing exam results, etc.

And the King of glory shall come in to destroy all forces of wandering thoughts about sickness. "Who is this King of glory? The LORD of hosts, he is the King of glory. Selah."

(Repeat this as many times as you want).

"Who is this King of glory? The LORD of hosts, he is the King of glory. Selah."

(Repeat this as many times as you want).

Additional Prayers on the Mind

O God, please let the spirit in Your word be always activated to operate in my mind in the name of Jesus.

O God, please help me to always arrest any strange

thought of my mind early before it settles in the name of Jesus.

Holy Father, please enable me to always check my conscience in the name of Jesus.
Father, Lord, please deliver my mind in Jesus' name.
I reject every thought that is not of God in the name of Jesus.

Thank You God for answered prayers.

Chapter 16

SEEKING RELEVANT INFORMATION FROM GOD

Please do an aggressive praise and worship before you do these prayers, and do not forget to pray for forgiveness of sins.

Do not dwell and die in ignorance of the truth. Seek to know the truth from God. Allow Him to reveal this to You Himself. Learn to hear from God.

There are places in the Bible where He invited us to come to Him to seek for information: Matthew 7:7–8; Isaiah 43:25–26; Isaiah 45:19b; etc.

In Deuteronomy 4:29, He says "But if from thence thou shalt seek the LORD your God, thou shalt find him, if thou seek him with all thy heart, and with all thy soul."

God is awesome, and when we seek relevant information from Him, we need to come before Him in fasting, holiness, and reverence; confessing all our sins, and pleading for forgiveness. We need to give Him thanks for all He has already done in our lives. Then we can present our requests before Him in faith, praying with concentration and with all our hearts. When you receive the revelation, thank Him and act on it without delay; for Jesus said, "Blessed are they that hear the word of God and keep it."

PRAYERS:
Deuteronomy 29:29 "The secret things belong unto the LORD our God: but those things which are revealed, belong unto us and to our children forever, that we may do all the words of this law.
Everlasting Father of all knowledge, please reveal to me the secret information pertaining to --- (Fill in what you want to know).

Daniel 2:22
"He revealeth the deep and secret things: he knoweth what is in the darkness, and the light dwelleth with him."
O Holy God of truth, please reveal to me the truth about --- to always enable me to live in obedience to Your word in the name of Jesus.

Psalm 25:14
"The secret of the LORD is with them that fear him; and he will shew them his covenant."
Most merciful God to whom secret knowledge belongs, I live in fear of You; please give me an insight into the secret surrounding this problem of --- in Jesus' name.

Matthew 7:7
"Ask, and it shall be given you; seek, and ye shall find;

knock, and it shall be opened unto you."

Father Lord, Your words are 'Yea' and 'Amen' to Your glory alone. Please I am desperately seeking for the right information about ---. Out of Your mercy, please reveal this information to me, so that I will be guided to make the right decision in the name of Jesus.

Joel 2:28

"And it shall come to pass afterward, that I will pour out my spirit upon all flesh, your sons and daughters shall prophesy, your old men shall dream dreams, and your young men shall see visions."

Most blessed Spirit of the living God, please impart on us the spirit of wisdom, knowledge, and prophesy, so that we can have the right knowledge about any matter that will guide us in the name of Jesus.

Ephesians 5:13

"But all things that are reproved are made manifest by the light: for whatsoever makes manifest is light."

Let Your light, O Lord, expose to us the secret knowledge we are seeking for in the name of Jesus.

Ephesians 3:3

"How that by revelation he made known unto me the mystery; as I wrote afore in few words."

Holy God, the Author of truth, please make known to me, by revelation, the mystery surrounding the information I need in Jesus' name.

Galatians 1:12

"For I neither receive it of man, nor was I taught it; but by the revelation of Jesus Christ."

Holy Lord Jesus Christ, any sin in my life that is responsible for my not receiving easily from you, please let your precious blood wash it away.

Daniel 2:47

"The king answered unto Daniel and said, of a truth it is, that your God is the God of gods and a Lord of kings, and a revealer of secrets, seeing thou couldest reveal this secret."

Holy God of wisdom, knowledge, and understanding, please bestow on me the power to receive, understand, and interpret the word of wisdom and knowledge in the name of Jesus.

Philippians 3:15

"Let us therefore, as many as be perfect, be thus minded: and if in anything ye be otherwise minded, God shall reveal even this unto you."

Our Father and our God, please let any revelation we receive come with understanding and power in the name of Jesus. Whenever we are in doubt, in ignorance, or being misled, please alert us, and lead us back to the truth that we are seeking in the name of Jesus.

Job 11:5–6

"But oh that God would speak, and open his lips against thee; and that he would show thee the secrets of wisdom, that they are double to that which is!"

Eternal Redeemer, we look forward to Your continued revelation of Your secrets about Your word and our lives, so that we shall work carefully and in truth in the name of Jesus.

Psalm 94: 9, 12 "He that planted the ear, shall he not hear? He that formed the eye, shall he not see?... Blessed is the man whom thou chastenest, O LORD, and teachest him out of thy law; that thou mayest give him rest from the days of adversity, until the pit be digged for the wicked." Your revelations, O mighty God, are right, instructive, corrective, give spiritual growth. Please have mercy and reveal to me now the secret reason for this matter in the name of Jesus.

Job 33:14–16
"For God speaketh once, yea twice, yet man perceiveth it not. In a dream, in a vision of the night, when deep sleep falleth upon men, in slumberings upon the bed; Then He openeth the ears of men, and sealeth their instruction." Father God, to whom secret knowledge belongs, please in Your mercy give me the grace to always understand and make use of every revelation I receive from you in the name of Jesus.

Daniel 2:29
"As for thee O king, thy thoughts came into thy mind upon thy bed, what should come to pass hereafter, and he that revealeth secrets, maketh known to thee what shall come to pass."

O Holy God, to whom all secrets are known, please make known to me what this problem means and how to go about it, in order to prevent it happening in Jesus' name.

Isaiah 45:18b–19
"I am the Lord, and there is none else, I have not spoken in secret, in a dark place of the earth: I said not unto the seed of Jacob, Seek ye me in vain: I the Lord speak righteousness, I declare things that are right."
Our Holy Father and our God, surely, we shall not seek You in vain for every word that proceeds from You enlightens. It is life and it is spirit. Please as me ask for enlightenment on relevant issues, let me receive information that will lead me away from that problem and sin in the name of Jesus.

.

Isaiah 43:25–26
"I, even I, am he that blotteth out thy transgressions, for mine own sake, and will not remember thy sins, Put me in remembrance; let us plead together".
Most merciful and understanding Father we are sinners, and sometimes the sinful nature of our minds seem to block our understanding. Please always reveal to me what I am asking in the way that we can understand it in the name of Jesus.

Chapter 17

PRAYERS FOR THE SANCTIFICATION OF A NEW HOUSE

Praise and Worship
Thanksgiving
Confession of Sins

PRAYERS:
Leviticus 14:52
"And he shall cleanse the house with the blood of the bird, and with running water." The blood of Jesus has replaced the blood of animals.
Hebrews 9:22a
"And almost all things are by the law purged with blood."
Hebrews 9:14 reads
"How much more shall the blood of Christ, who through the eternal Spirit offered himself without spot to God, purge your conscience from dead works to serve the living God."
I sprinkle the blood of Jesus on every part of this building and on the grounds in the name of Jesus. Go around the

house and sprinkle the blood by faith.

Revelations 12:11 reads
"And they overcame him by the blood of the Lamb, and by the word of their testimony".
Father God, please let the blood of Jesus flush out everything that rebels or challenges what Christ stands for in this house and compound in the name of Jesus. I claim by faith the victory of Jesus at the Cross in Jesus Name.

Hebrews 12:24 reads:
"And to Jesus the mediator of the new covenant, and to the blood of sprinkling, that speaketh better things than that of Abel."
O God of Abraham, Isaac, and Jacob, please let the power in the blood of Jesus silence any satanic voice crying out for sacrifice on this land, where the house is located, in the name of Jesus.

Numbers 23:23 reads
"Surely there is no enchantment against Jacob, neither is there any divination against Israel: according to this time it shall be said of Jacob and Israel, what hath God wrought!"
O Holy God of Deliverance, please let any satanic prayers of enchantment and incantations made on the grounds of this house before it was built be cancelled by the blood of Jesus in Jesus' name.

Matthew 15:13 reads:

"But he answered and said, Every plant, which my heavenly Father hath not planted, shall be rooted up."

O Holy God, whose words are 'Yea' and 'Amen' let anything that has been bewitched in this house, receive immediate deliverance in the name of Jesus.

Amos 9:3–4 reads:

"And though they hide themselves in the top of Carmel, I will search and take them out thence; and though they be hid from my sight at the bottom of the sea, thence will I command the serpent, and he shall bite them: And though they go into captivity before their enemies, thence will I command the sword, and it shall slay them: and I will set mine eyes upon them for evil, and not for good."

O Holy God of battle, Jehovah Nissi, please let any gateway of hell and the habitation of evil spirits on the grounds of this house receive Your righteous judgement and be uprooted in the name of Jesus.

Revelations 3:7

"These things saith he that is holy, He that is true, he that hath the key of David, he that openeth, and no man shutteth: and shutteth, and no man openeth."

O God, ever Faithful and Truthful, please let any door which Your hand of power has opened in this house remain permanently opened, and let any door You have shut, remain shut for ever in the name of Jesus.

Psalm 27:2

"When the wicked, even mine enemies and my foes, came upon me to eat up my flesh, they stumbled and fell."

Everlasting Warrior, to whom belongs glory, please let any enemy human or spiritual that may arise against the ownership of this property stumble and fall permanently in the name of Jesus.

John 1:4–5

"In him was life; and the life was the light of men. And the light shineth in the darkness, and the darkness comprehended it not."

O Holy God of light, please let any power of darkness operating in this house and compound be flushed out by Your light in the name of Jesus.

As you move around the four corners of the house, lay the palm of your hand on them, and declare this as you do so: "I possess this house in the name of Jesus." (You can substitute the name of the person you are praying for).

Psalm 91:9

"Because thou hast made the LORD, which is thy refuge, even the most High, thy habitation; there shall no evil befall thee, neither shall any plague come nigh thy dwelling."

Most blessed Spirit of the living God, please lead me on the path of obedience and holiness to Your word, so that evil will not locate this house in the name of Jesus.

Exodus 12:13

"And the blood shall be to you for a token upon the houses where you are: and when I see the blood, I will pass over you".

Anoint all the doors and windows of the house with the blood of Jesus, both inside and outside. Then pray:

Everlasting Deliverer, please let the foundation of this house be soaked in the blood of Jesus in the name of Jesus (several times).

Psalm 18:44–45

"As soon as they hear of me, they shall obey me: the strangers shall submit themselves unto me. The strangers shall fade away, and be afraid out of their close places."

The Holy God Almighty, who sees in the secret and in the open, in the spiritual and in the physical, please let any stranger hiding in any part of this house be permanently chased away by Your fire in the name of Jesus.

Matthew 15:13 reads:

"But he answered and said, Every plant, which my heavenly Father hath not planted, shall be rooted up."

Everlasting Father of all mercies, please let any evil plantation on the grounds of this house, that is responsible for financial devouring, stagnancy, and backwardness receive immediate challenge by Your fire and the blood of Jesus, and be permanently dislodged in Jesus' name.

Matthew 18:18 reads:

"Verily I say unto you, Whatsoever you shall bind on

earth shall be bound in heaven: and whatsoever ye shall loose on earth shall be loosed in heaven."

I take authority, in the name of Jesus, over anything that has been programmed by satanic powers to challenge the will of God in this house. By faith in the name of Jesus, I bind you, I paralyse you, and cast you into the uninhabitable places in the name of Jesus.

Job 22:28

"Thou shalt also decree a thing, and it shall be established unto thee: and light shall shine upon thy ways."

According to this scripture, I decree that this property will not generate debt or attract poverty into my life in the name of Jesus.

You, my property, I decree that you will not be the habitation of marine witchcraft, occults, and foundational enemies, both human and spiritual, in the name of Jesus (2 Corinthians 6:14–17).

You, this property, it is written that children are a heritage of the Lord, the fruit of the womb is His reward (Psalm 127:3). Therefore, you will not retard or delay pregnancy and child birth, steal any child, nor permit any demon to enter this house in the name of Jesus..

You, this property, Jesus has shed his blood for me and as a result, I owe you no blood in the name of Jesus (Ephesians 1:7).

You, this property, Jesus is the door and gateway into you; therefore, every other door and gateway is closed in Jesus Name. (John 14:6).

You, this property, you shall recover everything that the

enemy has stolen from me in the name of Jesus (Joel 2 :25–26).

You, this property, you will not work against me nor retard the destiny of God in my life in the name of Jesus.

Psalm 1:5

"Therefore the ungodly shall not stand in the judgement, nor sinners in the congregation of the righteous."

O Holy God, my Father, please do not let this house be a venue for planning evil in the name of Jesus. Let every plan of the enemy to establish a satanic stronghold in this house fail permanently in the name of Jesus.

Concluding Prayers

Almighty God of war and wonders, please let any power, spirit, or human assigned to oppose the will of God in this house fail permanently in the name of Jesus.

O Holy God, the Fountain of living waters, please let this house glorify You and let Your will be perfected in everything done in it in the name of Jesus.

Please God, let the blood of Jesus be a covering and a shelter in this house against satanic spirits in the name of Jesus.

Psalm 24:7

"Lift up your heads O ye gates; and be ye lift up, you everlasting doors (of this house); and the King of glory shall come in."

O holy King of Glory, please come into this property with all Your powers and occupy and be glorified in it, in the name of Jesus.

Then finally anoint all the doors and windows with anointing oil.

Cover the prayers with the blood of Jesus, and thank God for answered prayers, in Jesus' name.

Chapter 18

THE SPIRIT OF FEAR

There are many things that can give rise to fear, which the enemy uses as a weapon against man. These include: lies, threats, ill health, poverty, failure, environment, persecution, wars, etc. Fear gives rise to worry. The Word of God in Matthew 6:25 has warned that no one should worry about anything no matter how bad the situation may seem. Romans 8:35 states: "Who shall separate us from the love of Christ? Shall tribulation, or distress, or persecution, or famine, or nakedness, or peril, or sword?" Fear wars against faith and the love of God. It is; therefore, against what salvation is all about and should be rejected at all costs. As we repose our confidence in You, O God, please let Your name always be glorified in every situation in Jesus' name.

These prayers are put together to enable us defeat this spirit of fear.

Prayers
2 Timothy 1:7 reads:
"For God hath not given us a spirit of fear; but of power, and of love, and of a sound mind."

O Holy God, the Strength of our lives, please enable us to use these graces to overcome the spirit of fear in the name of Jesus.

1 John 4:18 reads:
"There is no fear in love, but perfect love casteth out fear, because fear has torment. He that feareth is not made perfect in love."
Everlasting Father, please let my life of faith in Your power to defeat all evils be completely free of fear in the name of Jesus. Let Your love which I received from Christ be able to banish fear from my life. I refuse to harbour the torment of fear in my heart in the name of Jesus.

Psalm 27:1 reads:
"The Lord is my light and my salvation; whom shall I fear? the LORD is the strength of my life of whom shall I be afraid?"
Light shines and darkness cannot comprehend it; and the spirit of fear cannot defeat the Lord in my life. Therefore, Father, God, please I refuse to tolerate it. Let it flee from my life in Jesus' name.

Psalm 27:3 reads:
"Though an host my encamp against me, my heart shall not fear: though war should rise against me, in this I will be confident."
As I dwell and grow daily in the knowledge and understanding of Your word, O Holy God, please let every spirit of fear be permanently ejected from my life

in the name of Jesus.

Psalm 27:13–14 reads:
"I had fainted, unless I believed to see the goodness of the LORD in the land of the liv-ing. Wait on the LORD: be of good courage, and he shall strengthen your heart. wait, I say, on the Lord."
O Holy God, our Strength and Salvation, as I wait on You in prayers, please always strengthen my resolve and courage to overcome any fear that will try to arise in my life in the name of Jesus.

Psalm 23:4 reads:
"Yea, though I walk through the valley of the shadow of death I will fear no evil;
for thou art with me; thy rod and thy staff they comfort me."
Holy God, the Habitation of our hope, please as problems arise, let me not fear, but abide even on a higher level of faith because Your comforting presence is always around us in Jesus' name.

Psalm 91:5–6 reads:
"Thou shalt not be afraid for the terror by night; nor of the arrow that flieth by day; Nor of the pestilence that walketh in the darkness; nor of the destruction that wasteth at noonday."
O Holy God, to whom alone belong all the power, please let me live to fear only You, my Creator, and not the wickedness of man in Jesus' name.

Proverbs 1:33

"But whoso hearkeneth unto me shall dwell safely, and shall be quiet from fear of evil."

O God, our Refuge in times of trouble, please let Your grace bestow upon me the spirit of obedience to Your word, so that I will not have to fear any evil in the name of Jesus.

Psalm 64:1 reads:

"Hear my voice, O God, in my prayer; preserve my life from fear of the enemy."

O Holy God of compassion and mercy, please whenever the enemy attacks and I pray, please answer me so that my faith will be strengthened in Jesus' name.

Psalm 56:11 reads:

"In God have I put my trust: I will not be afraid what man can do unto me."

O Holy God of power, as I trust in You and focus on Your power and love, please let the spirit of fear finally depart from my life in Jesus' name.

Psalm 46:1–2 reads:

"God is our refuge and strength, a very present help in trouble. Therefore will not we fear, though the earth be removed, and though the mountains be carried into the midst of the sea".

O mighty God of war, Your protection is a reliable stronghold no matter how severe the attack proves, please let Your ability to overcome strengthen my faith in Jesus' name.

Psalm 46:10 reads:
"Be still and know that I am God: I will be exalted among the heathen, I will be exalted in the earth."
Thank You, Holy God, our victorious Warrior, for exposing and destroying the satanic tactics of fear at the Cross. May all fear vanish as we claim our salvation in Jesus' name.

Isaiah 35:4 reads:
"Say to them that are of a fearful heart, Be strong, fear not: behold, your God will come with vengeance even God with a recompense; He will come and save you."
The very true and faithful God, please may my faith not be shaken as I wait patiently for you to come and recompense for me in Jesus' name.

Isaiah 8:13 reads:
"Sanctify the LORD of hosts himself; and let him be your fear, and let him be your dread."
O Holy God, our strong Tower, may we not fear man, but live to bestow all our fear and reverence on You alone in Jesus' name.

Psalm 118:6 reads:
"The Lord is on my side; I will not fear. What can man do unto me?"
O God, our Shelter and our Guide, please give me the grace to continuously abide in Your ways without any

fear of the enemy in Jesus' name.

Matthew 14:30–31 reads:
"But when he saw the wind boisterous, he was afraid; and beginning to sink, he cried saying, Lord, save me. And immediately Jesus stretched forth his hand and caught him, and said to him, O thou of little faith, wherefore didst thou doubt?"
O God, please have mercy on my doubt and weaknesses, and guide me by your mercy to an acceptable level of faith in Jesus' name.

Chapter 19

PRAYER AGAINST THE SATANIC SPIRIT OF DEATH AND HELL

Pray these prayers with all seriousness and concentration. Psalm 118:17 reads:

"I shall not die, but live, and declare the works of the LORD."

Our Holy God that has the key of death and hell, please let me not die, but live to declare and do Your work in the land of the living in Jesus' name. Let the wicked devices of the enemy to terminate my life fail in Jesus' name.

Isaiah 54:15 reads:

"Behold they shall surely gather together, but not by me; whosoever shall gather together against thee shall fall for thy sake."

O Holy God whose words are 'Yea' and 'Amen' to Your glory, please let every death threat against me fail permanently for my sake in the name of Jesus.

Psalm 69:14–15 reads:

"Deliver me out of the mire, and let me not sink: let me be delivered from them that hate me, and out of the deep waters."

Everlasting Redeemer, in Thy loving kindness and mercy, please make me escape from all the destructive moves of the enemy in Jesus' name.

Psalm 27:2 reads:

"When the wicked, even mine enemies and my foes, came upon me to eat up my flesh, they stumbled and fell."

Jehovah Nisi, the mighty God of battle, please let any unrepentant enemy that has planned my death stumble and fall permanently in the name of Jesus.

Proverbs 26:27 reads:

"Whoso diggeth a pit shall fall therein; and he that rolleth a stone, it will return upon him."

Let my enemies receive Your righteous judgement in Jesus' name.

Romans 8:2 reads:

"For the law of the Spirit of life in Christ Jesus hath made me free from the law of sin and death."

The Holy God, our Light and Salvation, since the leading of the Holy Spirit sets a man apart from sin, please strengthen me in my determination to walk in the path of right-eousness, so that I can make the Kingdom in Jesus' name.

Isaiah 28:18 reads:

"And your covenant with death shall be disannulled, and your agreement with hell shall not stand".

The Holy God of deliverance, because the blood of Jesus has broken every satanic cove-nant in our lives, please let any covenant made by my ancestors become null and void in my life. Let the foundation of the Lord Jesus replace any satanic foundation in my life in Jesus' name.

Romans 8:11 reads:

"But if the Spirit of him that raised up Jesus from the dead dwell in you, he that raised up Christ from the dead shall also quicken your mortal bodies by his Spirit that dwelleth in You."

Most blessed Holy Spirit of the living God, please release Your breath of life into my mortal body in the name of Jesus.

Romans 8:26 reads:

"Likewise the Spirit also helpeth our infirmities; for we know not what we should pray for as we ought; but the Spirit itself maketh intercession for us with groaning which can-not be uttered."

Holy Spirit, please in Your mercy, kindly intercede for me, so that God can cancel any threat of death on my life in Jesus' name.

Psalm 6:4–5 reads:

"Return, O LORD, deliver my soul: Oh save me for thy mercies' sake. For in death there is no remembrance of thee; in the grave who shall give thee thanks?"

O most merciful and able God, please let the victory of Your beloved Son Jesus Christ triumph again over any premature spirit of death and hell in my life in Jesus' name.

Mark 16:18 reads:

"And if they drink any deadly thing, it shall not hurt them".

O holy covenant-keeping God, please do not let me perish from deadly intake of whatev-er may be forced on me in ignorance; and do not let me be initiated, even in my dreams, in Jesus' name.

Psalm 94:17 reads:

"Unless the Lord had been my help, my soul had almost dwelt in silence."

Father, God, You are the God that reverses adverse situations and delivers the helpless; it is only our faith in this act of mercy that has kept us going. Please do not let this faith be in vain in Jesus' name.

Isaiah 49:25 reads:

"But thus said the LORD; Even the captives of the mighty shall be taken away; and the prey of the terrible shall be delivered."

Jehovah Elshaddai, You are the mighty God in battle, please command deliverance for me and all those under threat of death that we may be delivered from our enemies in Jesus' name.

Psalm 18:4–5 reads:

"The sorrows of death compassed me, and the floods of ungodly men made me afraid. The sorrows of hell compassed me about; the snares of death prevented me. In my dis-tress I called upon the LORD, and cried unto my God: he heard my voice out of his temple."

Jehovah Nissi, the mighty God in battle, please command the wickedness of my enemies to be suddenly terminated. Let them turn their backs and flee; for by strength shall no man prevail, in Jesus' name.

Psalm 35:7 reads:

"For without cause have they hid for me their net in a pit, which without cause they dug for my soul."

O God, the great Deliverer, please let Your whirlwind drive away all our unrepentant en-emies, and let all their satanic plans be turned upside down in Jesus' name.

Psalm 37:14 read:

"The wicked have drawn out the sword, and have bent their bow, to cast down the poor and needy, and to slay such as be of upright conversation."

O God, please disappoint all the devices of the enemy, so that they cannot perform their evil enterprises; and command the satanic spirit of death and hell to bow out of my life in Jesus' name.

Psalm 34:19–20 reads:

"Many are the afflictions of the righteous: but the Lord delivereth him out of them all. He keepeth all his bones:

not one of them is broken."

O God, please speak failure and permanent defeat to the aggressive attacks of the enemy against me. Do not let any of my bones be broken in Jesus' name.

Proverbs 9:11 reads:

"For by me thy days shall be multiplied, and the years of thy life shall be increased."

The everlasting God of mercy, who extends days and multiplies years, please do not let the enemy shorten my years of life in Jesus' name.

O God, arise and let Your enemies (my enemies) be scattered in Jesus' name. Let all those who, through fear of death, were all their lives unwillingly in bondage to Satan receive deliverance in Jesus' name.

Thank You, Holy God, for answered prayers in Jesus' name.

Chapter 20

PRAY FOR THE WORD

Holy Father, God, we thank You for Your word, for it is life to us in Jesus' name.

John 15:7 reads:
"If ye abide in me, and my words abide in you, ye shall ask what ye will, and it shall be done unto you."
O Holy God of our salvation, please let all Christians who are currently in serious bondage of sin, because of lack of the knowledge and understanding of the Word, be helped to receive Your word, and come to salvation in the name of Jesus.

- God, please let Your word become a hedge of fire around us in Jesus' name.
- Holy God, please let Your word be spoken with boldness and assurance in Jesus' name.
- God, let Your word breakdown every iron heart in Jesus' name.
- Please let Your word banish the spirit of fear from its bearers in Jesus' name.
- Holy God, please make the bearers of Your word

selfless in Jesus' name.

•   O God, please let all those who are contending with Your word in our lives fail permanently in Jesus' name.

•   Please let the hunger for souls overshadow the bearers of Your word in Jesus' name.

•   Father Lord, please empower the bearers of Your word to endure persecution in Jesus' name.

•   O God please, let a time come when the front pages of every paper in the world will carry Your word in Jesus' name.

•   Holy God of knowledge, please let the hearers of Your word never forget it in Jesus' name.

•   God, please let every hearer of Your word receive life in Jesus' name.

•   Father, Lord, please let Your word release the spirit of genuine repentance in Jesus' name.

•   Please let the hearts of the hearers of Your word be permanently turned to Your word in Jesus' name

•   Please God, let Your word stand as the light in the hearts of those who receive it, in the name of Jesus.

•   Please God, please let Your word challenge and uproot from people every evil plantation that make them to resist it in Jesus' name.

•   Please God, please let the hunger for Your word be immensely increased in the world today in Jesus' name.

•   Please let Your word always overcome all the forces of resistance against it in Jesus' name.

•   God, please let Your plans for Your word be more than fulfilled in the lives of both the preachers and hearers in Jesus' name.

• Please Father let Your word cut through the inner most parts of the hearts that hear it, in Jesus' name.

• Please let it bring peace and unity to the church and in our families, in Jesus' name.

• Everlasting Father, please let Your word turn the hearts that rejected You back to You again in Jesus' name.

• Our Father and our God, please let Your word completely overcome the demons of mammon in Jesus' name.

• Holy Lord, please let Your word be accompanied with a genuine fear of You in Jesus' name.

• God, please do not allow the relevance of Your word to diminish in the hearts of those who have received it in Jesus' name.

• Holy God, please let Your word impart grace to the hearers in Jesus' name.

• Father Lord, please let it be spoken with love and humility in Jesus' name.

• Holy God, please let Your word bring comfort to the hearers in Jesus' name.

• Father Lord, please let Your word become fire, challenge, and overcome all Your enemies in the name of Jesus.

• Holy God, please let all the sicknesses, diseases, illnesses, and infirmities interfering with the spread of Your word be made to return to their sources in the name of Jesus.

• Father God, please let the spirit in Your word be activated to always operate in the lives of the hearers in

Jesus' name.

- Father, Lord, please expand the channels of disseminating Your word in Jesus' name.

- Holy Father, God, please do not let the bearers of Your word labour in vain in Jesus' name.

- Father, Lord, please renew the zeal and the strength of the bearers of Your word in Jesus' name.

- Father, Lord, please create greater opportunities for the bearers of Your word in Jesus' name

- God, please empower the preachers of Your word to speak Your word in their dreams in Jesus' name.

- God, please let all forces of darkness succumb to Your word in Jesus' name.

- Father Lord, please let the light of Your word shine in every city of the world in Jesus' name.

- Holy God, please let all hospitals, prisons, rehabilitation centres, camps, etc., re-echo Your word in Jesus' name.

- God, please let the power in Your word be felt in every heart that hears it in the name of Jesus.

- Our Father and our God, please let Your word always provide answers to the immediate needs of the hearers in Jesus' name.

- Please let Your word always overcome any immediate resistance to it in Jesus' name.

- Please let Your word always convince the hearers in Jesus' name.

- God, please let Your word always release a hunger for holiness in the lives of the hearers in Jesus' name.

- God, please let Your word always minister the

implications of sin to the hearers in Jesus' name.

- Holy God, please let Your word be acknowledged as the only final solution to any problem in Jesus' name.

- Holy God, please let Your word always impart love, comfort, and bring hope into the hearts of the hearers in Jesus' name.

- Holy Father, please let it release the empowerment to strive for holiness, in Jesus' name.

- God, please let Your word be a great encouragement, not discouragement, to the hearers in Jesus' name.

- God, please let all those bearing Your word with immorality be seriously put right in the name of Jesus.

- God, please let Your word penetrate into every evil foundation and deliver it in Jesus' name.

- Please Father, let Your word always minister continuity to the hearts of the hearers in Jesus' name.

- God, please let Your word become highly interesting and revealing to the hearers in Jesus' name.

- God, please let Your word always address the immediate needs of the hearers in Jesus' name.

- Holy God, please let the power in Your word always draw the hearers back to it, like a magnet, in Jesus' name.

- God, please let Your word break every stumbling block against it in Jesus' name.

- Holy God, please let it minister immediate deliverance to the hearers in Jesus' name.

- Holy Father, God, please let the spirits behind Your word operate in the lives of the hearers in the name

of Jesus.

• Holy Father, God, please let the bearers of Your word always communicate further instructions about Your word to its hearers in Jesus' name.

• Holy God, please let the bearers of Your word be covered by the blood of Jesus in Jesus' name.

• Holy Father, please do not allow any bearer of Your word to perish in this work in Jesus' name.

• Holy Father, God, please protect the families of the bearers of Your word in Jesus' name.

• My holy Father and my God, please let Your word silence all objections in Jesus' name.

• Holy Father, God, please let Your word always be received with happiness and appreciation in Jesus' name.

• Holy God, please let the time come when all doctors will administer drugs with Your word on their lips in Jesus' name.

• Holy Father, God, please, through Your word, increase immensely the number of miracles among patients whom doctors have given up hope on in Jesus' name.

• Father Lord, please make us to realize that Your word should be pronounced in holiness in Jesus' name.

• Father Lord, please sanctify Your word in our mouths in Jesus' name.

• Holy Father, please let our thoughts always be on Your word in Jesus' name.

• Holy Father, God, please empower us never to distort the meaning in Your word in Jesus' name.

• God, please help us to learn something useful

from Your word, every day, in Jesus' name.

• Father God, please empower us to live Your word every day in Jesus' name.

• Please, Holy God, empower us to meditate on Your word every day in Jesus' name.

• Please let the benefits of knowing and living Your word not depart from us in Jesus' name.

• Holy God, please give us the power to always render a good explanation of Your word, clearly, to unbelievers in Jesus' name.

• God, please let Your word be a mediator of the current crisis and wars going on in the world in Jesus' name.

• Father, God, please let Your word reproduce at a faster rate in Jesus' name.

• God, please let all schools and institutions teach and live Your word in Jesus' name.

• God, anoint Your word to penetrate forbidden areas and at an alarming speed in Jesus' name.

• Holy God, please let Your word purge the hearts of the hearers in Jesus' name.

• God, please let all those who cannot afford to purchase the Bible receive them as gifts in Jesus' name.

• Holy God, please let all the promises in Your word be manifested in the lives of the hearers as an encouragement in Jesus' name.

• God, please do not let the bearers of Your word be in want in Jesus' name.

• Please let the enemy be defeated in all arguments over Your words in Jesus' name.

- Holy Father, God, please let the impossible become possible to the hearers of Your word in Jesus' name.

- Holy God, please teach the bearers of Your word the most effective way to minister it in Jesus' name.

- God, please let Your word do more than it is doing at the moment in Jesus' name.

- God, please let the confidence in Your word be immensely increased in Jesus' name.

- Please, let the enemies of the Word, who attack the bearers of the Word, always fail, permanently, in Jesus' name.

- Please, let Your word minister immediate revival to the world in Jesus' name.

- God, please let those who minister Your word also learn from their ministrations in Jesus' name

- Please may the bearers of Your word never speak it in shame in Jesus' name

- God, please may the afflicted and every one find comfort in Your word in Jesus' name.

- Holy God, please turn the hearts of all your children towards the Word, so that they will not backslide in Jesus' name.

- Almighty and everlasting Father, please let all the spiritual powers attacking Your word in the lives of Your children fail permanently in the name of Jesus.

- Holy God, please let Your word release the spirit of concentration for the hearers in Jesus' name.

- God, please sanctify every heart that receives Your word in Jesus' name.

- God, please let Your breath continually disseminate Your word all over the world in Jesus' name.
- Holy Father, please let the whole ministration of Your word be covered by the blood of Jesus in Jesus' name.
- Please let Your spiritual messengers accompany all ministers of Your word in Jesus' name.
- God, please let the glorious ray of the gospel shine on every heart that hears Your word in Jesus' name.
- most merciful God, please let Your word be always ministered with a spirit of humility in Jesus' name.
- Holy God, please always silence all distractions that may arise spreading Your word in Jesus' name.
- God, please sanctify our breath and mouth as we minister Your word in Jesus' name.
- Holy God, please always sanctify the sights where the gospel is preached in the name of Jesus.
- Holy God, please let the spirit of slumber be put away from the lives of those who listen to Your word in Jesus' name.
- God, please grant the bearers of the word a retentive memory for all they have to say in the name of Jesus.
- Holy Father, our God, please let all the strangers trying to disrupt the growth of the gospel fail permanently in Jesus' name.
- God, please let the Word be deeply rooted in the whole world in Jesus' name.
- God, please let Your word do exploits for You; bringing revival to the world in the name of Jesus.

- God, please let the heart of all the people all over the world be receptive to the Word, its growth, and benefits in the name of Jesus.
- God, please let the feeling of curiosity and the fear of God overshadow any opposition to the word, in the name of Jesus.
- God, please let Your word go forth like fire and win souls for You all over the world in the mighty name of Jesus.
- Our holy Father and our God, please let the foundational powers attacking the gospel of our Lord Jesus Christ always fail, permanently, in Jesus' name.
- Holy God, please let Your word become fire and chase away all oppositions in the mighty name of Jesus.
- Mighty God, please let the efforts of the enemies of the gospel to overthrow the bearers of the Word fail and be permanently frustrated in the name of Jesus.
- God, please let any gate of hell militating against the growth of the Word be shut permanently in the name Jesus.
- Everlasting Father, please make our enemies subject to the Word in the name of Jesus.
- Father, Lord, please let the gospel of our Lord Jesus Christ be deeply rooted in all hearts in the name of Jesus.
- God, please make Your word to become the focal point of all solutions in the world in Jesus' name.
- Lord, please reveal and teach Your children the hidden meaning in Your word in the name of Jesus.
- God, please let Your word become fire and speak

for You in the name of Jesus.

• Holy God, please let Your word break every yoke of foundational bondage in the name of Jesus.

• Father, Lord, please do not allow any bearer of the Word to be arrested or detained in any enemy camp in the name of Jesus.

• Father, Lord, please fill the bearers of Your word with fresh fire in Jesus' name.

• Holy Spirit, please sanctify the mouths of the bearers of Your word to win souls for You in Jesus' name.

• Father, Lord, please encourage all bearers of the gospel in the name of Jesus.

• Holy Father, please make available the resources needed for the effective propagation of the gospel in the name of Jesus.

• Holy Lord, please lead the bearers of the gospel to fertile grounds in the name of Jesus.

• My Father and my God, please always take care of the health and safety of the bearers of the gospel in Jesus' name.

• Father, Lord, please let the effectiveness of the gospel be felt everywhere in Jesus' name.

• God, please let no word of Yours spoken by Your servants fall to the ground in the name of Jesus.

• God, please let those who hear Your word never be the same again in Jesus' name.

• Father, Lord, please create more fertile grounds for the propagation of the gospel in the name of Jesus

• Father, Lord, please let Your spiritual workers ensure adequate and safe transportation for the propagation of the gospel in Jesus' name.

• Holy Lord, please protect the bearers of the gospel from spiritual and physical attacks and accidents in Jesus' name.

• Holy Spirit, please speak through the mouths of the bearers of the gospel in Jesus' name.

• Father, Lord, please let Your word break down and permanently overcome every yoke of the enemy in the name of Jesus.

• Father, Lord, please let all speakers of Your word always be sanctified in Jesus' name.

• Holy Spirit, please plant the word of God securely in the hearts of the hearers in Jesus' name.

• Holy Spirit, please let the hearers of the Word always have a good understanding and knowledge of the Word in Jesus' name. Let them always have something useful and interesting to remember in the name of Jesus.

• God, please let Your word always arrest the attention of the hearers in the name of Jesus.

• Father, Lord, please help the bearers of the Word to speak with understanding in Jesus' name.

• Father, Lord, please give the bearers of the Word the empowerment to preach to all and not to a selected few in the name of Jesus.

• Holy Spirit, please teach us to minister with love and compassion in Jesus' name.

• Father, Lord, please let the preachers of Your word always be well prepared for the work they are to do in Jesus' name.

• Father, Lord, please let the preachers of Your

word mirror the benefits of Your word in Jesus' name

• Holy God, please make the whole world feel a desperate need for Your gospel in Jesus' name.

• God, please let holiness and righteousness be the lot of the bearers of the gospel in the name of Jesus.

• Father, Lord, please protect the homes and relatives of the bearers of the gospel in the name of Jesus.

• Our holy Father and our God, please let Your word be followed by miracles, signs, and wonders in the name of Jesus.

• God, please remove distractions from the heart of the listeners and bearers of Your word in Jesus' name.

• Father, Lord, please do not let Your word give rise to any strife between the bearers and hearers in the name of Jesus

• God, please do not allow the bearers or hearers of Your word miss any good opportunities or any relevant point in the name of Jesus.

• God, please let the Word that proceed from the mouths of the bearers always be covered by the blood of Jesus in Jesus' name.

• Holy God, please give the hearers of Your word the grace to repent and manifest changed behaviours in the name of Jesus.

• Father, God, please let Your word pierce through the souls and spirits, bones and marrows of the hearers in Jesus' name.

• O God, please let Your word be a lamp unto the feet of the hearers in Jesus' name.

• O God, please let the spirit attached to Your word

never leave the hearers' hearts until they have achieved their purpose in Jesus' name.

- God, our Strength, please let Your word conquer the world for You in Jesus' name.

- Holy God, please let Your word speak immediate power and credibility to the hearers in Jesus' name.

- O God, please make the hearers to enjoy the word being spoken to them by the bearers of Your word in Jesus' name.

- Eternal Redeemer, please let the preachers minister with patience and endurance in the name of Jesus.

- Everlasting Father, please do not allow any sickness in the lives of those preaching Your word in Jesus' name.

- Holy Father, O God, please extend the scope of the bearers of the gospel in Jesus' name.

- O God, please let miracles, signs, and wonders always accompany the propagation of Your word in Jesus' name.

- Holy Spirit, please intercede for the success of the Word in Jesus' name.

- Holy Father, God, please let any opposition during the propagation of Your word be sorted out amicably in the name of Jesus.

- Father, Lord, please let Your word go with wisdom and the fear of You in Jesus' name.

- Father God, please let Your word minister immediate fruit of the womb to any barren woman who accepts it with faith in Jesus' name.

• Father God, please let Your word always minister faith and conviction to the hearers in Jesus' name.

• Holy God, please always assign Your spirit to teach every hearer of Your word in Jesus' name.

• O God please remove the spirit of slumber from the hearers in Jesus' name.

• Father, God, please draw the hearers of the word to the churches, and let the blood of redemption be a protection for them in the name of Jesus.

• Holy Father, I pray that you will use this book to reach out to all those with specific problems; who are truly in need of it, so that you can be glorified, in Jesus' name.

• Thank You, God, for answered prayers in Jesus' name.

Chapter 21

CONCLUSION

BIBLICAL PRINCIPLES

1.   The enemy who boasts that he almost did it knows not God, the Master Timer.

2.   Do not waste more time on an already wasted time.

3.   Focus on God, not on man, so that you do not lose out completely.

4.   The praises of God are safe and true but that of man is questionable.

5.   Best safety lies in guarding against sin every second of your life.

6.   It is not John or Jenny that is your worst enemy but sin.

7.   Allow holiness to drive away poverty from you.

8.   Anyone who steals the glory of God has already condemned himself.

9.   Wisdom is to allow God to make all the decisions for you and you abide in it.

10.   The sickness of AIDS and leprosy may not prevent

you from entering heaven, but sin definitely will.

11.   Satan fights through the praises of human beings.

12.   Success is not to base your trust in man.

13.   Sin is the only true terminal disease in man.

14.   Who is the richest? The holy and the righteous.

15.   Pride and unforgiveness render your tireless labour for God useless.

16.   The fear of Satan is a sure step towards failure.

17.   Self-condemnation is to hide a skeleton in the basket.

18.   Kingdom judgment may become a mystery and a shocker to many.

19.   Holiness, life, health, wealth, and protection are the graces of salvation.

20.   Anger is a silent intruder, destroyer, and a killer.

21.   Wickedness later begets much suffering and anguish.

22.   The act of backsliding is the beginning of failure.

23.   Life is to preserve your righteousness.

24.   Rely not on anything that proceeds from any mouth except the Word.

25.   Human interpretation lacks the truth of God's perspective.

26.   Sin, the surest gateway to suffering and deprivation.

27.   Go to Satan for help, and pay with the last drop of your blood.

28.   God will remember all unrepented sins though they belong in the past and is concealed.

29.   Wisdom is not to add or detract from the Word.

30.   Obedience to the Word goes with the fullness of

God.

31.   As the deceiver deceives, so is he subject to deceit.

32.   Before you complain about your sufferings, recount all your past sins.

33.   You can get out of the sins you know, but not the ones you do not know.

34.   Your true character is what you are concealing.

35.   Our strength in God lies in our obedience to Him.

36.   Let God find you relevant, not useless, in His scheme of things.

37.   If you always desire to slumber in bed of roses, your flesh will be meat for the enemy.

38.   If you value your sleep, you discredit your destiny.

39.   Let it not be said that in spite of all said and done, you were found wanting.

40.   Any exaggeration or embellishment of the Word is a deviation from the Word and the truth.

41.   The most common thing in humans is sin.

42.   True humility is to forget your rights and comfort.

43.   It is what you habitualize that remains in you whether sin or holiness.

44.   Guide well your dreams, for the devil never goes to sleep.

45.   The platform for satanic attack is the dream arena.

46.   The truly righteous gets more determined as the attack gets hotter.

47.   Any compromise in obedience is a deviation from God.

48.   The only refuge is of God.

49.   Boasting is not the way of the Kingdom.

50.   Best safety lies in righteousness.

51.   God's word cannot be substituted by man's.

52.   Just as service to God is highly rewarding, so is service to Satan a deadly loss.

53.   Striving to be noticed is of the devil.

54.   Only church membership cannot guarantee the Kingdom.

55.   Sin is to be repented and remitted, not concealed and repeated.

56.   God is the only Master Timer.

57.   Complaints and murmurings are a continuous displeasure to God.

58.   If you keep company, maintain your individuality.

59.   Faith is not to run away from the problem.

60.   If your enemy is also your confidant, you have a long period of suffering to contend with.

61.   The conclusion of the matter is not to leave this world as a sinner.

62.   Minor problems ignored escalate into major ones.

63.   Forgiveness goes hand in hand with forgetfulness.

64.   The Word is to be lived.

65.   Know the power in the Word, and speak only the Word.

66.   It is better to endure than to assume a prodigal stance.

67.   Any spirit of superiority leads to failure.

68.   Always aim at pleasing others before yourself.

69.   He who excels in holiness and righteousness,

excels in wealth.

70. Food is an indirect killer. What Eve ate averted man's destiny.

71. Politeness is not weakness.

72. Meekness is not weakness.

Ingram Content Group UK Ltd.
Milton Keynes UK
UKHW020624110523
421574UK00012B/315